MAXIMUM
MARKETING,
MINIMUM
DOLLARS

The Top 50 Ways to Grow
Your Small Business

KIM T. GORDON

KAPLAN PUBLISHING

This publication is designed to provide accurate and authoritative information in regard to the subject matter covered. It is sold with the understanding that the publisher is not engaged in rendering legal, accounting, or other professional service. If legal advice or other expert assistance is required, the services of a competent professional person should be sought.

President, Kaplan Publishing: Roy Lipner
Vice President and Publisher: Maureen McMahon
Acquisitions Editor: Karen Murphy
Senior Managing Editor: Jack Kiburz
Typesetter: the dotted i
Cover Designer: Design Literate, Inc.

Library of Congress Cataloging-in-Publication Data

Gordon, Kim T.
Maximum marketing, minimum dollars : the top 50 ways to grow your small business / Kim T. Gordon
   p.   cm.
   Includes index.
   ISBN-13: 978-1-4195-2002-0
   ISBN-10: 1-4195-2002-4
   1. Marketing—Management. 2. Small business—Marketing. I. Title.
   HF5415.13.G65   2006
   658.8—dc22

2005027672

PRAISE FOR *MAXIMUM MARKETING, MINIMUM DOLLARS*

"You can't afford to miss this definitive marketing guide. Its step-by-step approach to a comprehensive range of marketing tactics, along with the success stories of entrepreneurs nationwide, make it easy to follow and enjoyable to read. If you're serious about growing your business and increasing sales, this book shows you how."

—RIEVA LESONSKY, EDITORIAL DIRECTOR, *ENTREPRENEUR*

"Don't spend another dollar on marketing until you read Kim T. Gordon's latest book—Maximum Marketing, Minimum Dollars. *Her practical, no-nonsense advice and case studies are sure to save you money and reduce stress."*

**—JANE APPLEGATE, CONSULTANT AND AUTHOR OF
201 GREAT IDEAS FOR YOUR SMALL BUSINESS AND
*THE ENTREPRENEUR'S DESK REFERENCE***

"A treasure trove of practical, logical, and—best of all—money-making ideas! Maximum Marketing, Minimum Dollars *is aimed at small to medium businesses, but many marketing giants can profit from the wisdom Kim Gordon has packed into this book."*

—HERSCHELL GORDON LEWIS, AUTHOR AND MARKETING CONSULTANT

"This is the definitive guide to marketing for every business owner—whether starting or expanding a business. But what sets this book apart is that Kim T. Gordon gives you a guide for setting priorities and choosing the set of marketing tools that will be most effective for your business."

**—SHARON G. HADARY, EXECUTIVE DIRECTOR,
CENTER FOR WOMEN'S BUSINESS RESEARCH**

DEDICATION

Many thanks to all the small-business owners who shared their fascinating stories for this book. Your passion is contagious, and your marketing insights will help others achieve higher levels of success.

Contents

Ask small-business owners from Manhattan to San Francisco to name their number one goal, and they'll tell you their chief priority is to increase sales. The trouble is, while entrepreneurs are often terrific at operating their core businesses, most have little or no marketing experience or know-how. In fact, the Small Business Administration confirms the two biggest reasons for small-business failure are lack of effective marketing programs and undercapitalization. Not surprisingly, the two go hand in hand.

Maximum Marketing, Minimum Dollars: The Top 50 Ways to Grow Your Small Business is the small-business owner's guide to success on a budget. This comprehensive book focuses on a host of new tactics plus the latest updates on tried-and-true, low-cost marketing methods that are essential to increasing sales. Filled with more than 30 case histories of small businesses nationwide that have achieved success on a budget, it's a real-life look at today's most important marketing tactics. You'll find in-depth guidance on affordable ways to generate income quickly and fuel your sales. And you'll learn how to choose the right tactics to fit your unique needs and create a marketing program that you can manage along with the day-to-day operation of your growing business.

Many of the strategies and tactics in this book are employed by America's largest companies. But I'll show you how to take advantage of these methods without spending megabucks. In fact, all 50 of the tactics recommended are suitable for small businesses of just about any size, whether you have one employee or several hundred. And they're based on my 27 years in the field, constant immersion in the newest marketing data and study results—plus input from a cross section of the millions of small-business owners who read my magazine and online columns each month. Their questions and comments inform my writing and ensure this book contains the essential information you want most.

WHAT'S INSIDE *MAXIMUM MARKETING, MINIMUM DOLLARS?*

Chapter 1 kicks off with step-by-step guidance on creating an effective Web site, from choosing the best domain name and designing your site to successful e-commerce (including the ten factors that lead to solid online sales). Chapters 2 and 3 focus on online marketing tactics. You'll find help creating hardworking e-mail marketing programs, earning high rankings on search engines, and conducting affordable online advertising campaigns. These chapters also guide you to the newest resources for building your own opt-in marketing lists and in-house databases.

You don't need a publicist to get your company's name in the newspaper, you just need to know how to handle your own public relations. That's why Chapter 4 focuses on key aspects of PR, from establishing a media relations program, organizing your own events, and the hottest new ways to build buzz to harnessing a little "star power" to get attention. Next, Chapter 5 shows you how to use the latest out-of-home marketing vehicles, such as electronic billboards, and ways to save money by creating your own place-based marketing.

Sales letters and direct mail are the workhorses of small businesses. Getting them right without breaking the bank is the subject of Chapter 6, which demonstrates how marriage mail reduces direct-mail costs and shows you how to create a dimensional-mail campaign that gets past screeners. You'll also find extensive guidance on creating the perfect sales letter—without hiring a copywriter—including four sample letters.

Chapter 7 is all about relationship marketing. There's assistance in setting up your own referral program and in-depth information on ways to motivate your customers with a rewards program. Competitive alliances and partnership marketing, which dramatically reduce costs for small-business owners, are comprehensively explained in Chapter 8.

Chapter 9 shows you how to find and make the most of unique niche markets. It focuses on high-return marketing tactics, including the use of ethnic media. Low-cost takes on traditional tactics—including the new affordability of cable TV (yes, TV!), radio, and magazines—are the subject of Chapter 10, proving that many of today's smartest marketing tactics are now within reach of small businesses.

Did you know that a growing number of small-business owners are building sales to local audiences by taking their messages to the big screen with cinema advertising while spending significantly less than the cost of newspaper ads? This new media opportunity, along with experiential marketing (another high-ROI tactic that's been a well-kept secret of the Fortune 100), are revealed in Chapter 11. Chapter 12 rounds out this comprehensive book with a practical guide to creating your own marketing program using the 50 budget-wise tactics you've learned about.

As you can see, after reading *Maximum Marketing, Minimum Dollars*, you'll be ready to seamlessly implement a year-round marketing program for your own business that will increase sales—and won't break the bank.

The goal of this book is to arm you with 50 great, low-cost marketing tactics that you can put in place today to increase sales and grow your business. In addition, trumping the competition also means knowing how to brand and position your business by differentiating your products and services. For a marketing tactic to succeed, the message it conveys must resonate with—and motivate—prospects and customers. So before you begin learning how to successfully reach your target audience, let's take a quick look at a smart way to pinpoint your most important marketing message.

It's as simple as answering three fundamental questions:

1. What are the benefits of your product or service?
2. Who will want to buy it?
3. Why will they want to buy it from you?

Your answers to these basic questions will shape the central marketing themes you establish for your company, product, or service

You can answer the first question by defining the bottom-line benefits customers will enjoy when they choose to buy from you. Many small-business owners are unsure of the difference between a true customer benefit and what is, in fact, a "feature" or characteristic of your product or service. Benefits always answer the prospect's question, "What's in it for me?" And the benefits you claim must be different in some way from those marketed by your competitors to successfully differentiate your business and position it among a vast field of competition.

What sets your company or offer apart? It may be the way you provide your services, a unique aspect of your product, or even your method of delivery. But what matters most is that this benefit adds value and is desired by your target audience.

To find your bottom-line benefits, begin by making a comprehensive list of all the features of your company, its products, or services. You should expect your list to be fairly long—many small-business owners can name 25 to 30 features that describe what they market. When you look at your completed list, you'll see that groups of features have certain elements in common and equate to the same bottom-line benefit. Scan your long list of features and translate them into just four or five benefits that answer the question, "What's in it for me?" For example, suppose two of your features are "open until midnight on weekends" and "free local delivery." Both of these will relate to a single bottom-line customer benefit: convenience.

Once you've finalized your core benefits, you can make them the central theme of all your marketing messages and use them one-to-one with prospects in sales meetings and when networking. It's most helpful to create a single benefit statement, which is a one-sentence presentation of your company's principal benefits.

Here's an example:

> Customers of XYZ Company enjoy great savings and shopping convenience thanks to new, factory-direct pricing and longer hours of operation.

You'll note that the two up-front benefits (great savings and shopping convenience) are followed by two features (factory-direct pricing and longer hours), which explain the promised benefits. Just use the same procedure when including benefits in your marketing materials. In a company brochure, for instance, create your headlines and subheads incorporating important customer benefits and use features in the body copy to explain them.

Answering the second question—Who will want to buy what you market?—often proves tricky for new small-business owners. Your best bet is to look at the demographics (age, gender, household income, and so on) of the customers of your closest competitors. These are actually your most qualified prospects because they're actively purchasing similar products or services. Even if you're entering a new niche market or are the very first to launch a new type of product, you'll still need to examine the customers of other companies from which you hope to take market share.

It's always much easier to fill a need than to create one, so a potential customer who is purchasing a similar product or service is an excellent target for a company that can offer something more. The addition of a new benefit or promise of superior value is the principal reason someone will choose to buy from you. To answer question number three—Why will your customers want to buy your product or service?—take a long, hard look at your competition and the benefits they promise. Decide what makes your company your customers' best choice and build your marketing themes around this core advantage.

Get the idea? Now you're ready to use the 50 tactics in *Maximum Marketing, Minimum Dollars* to reach prospects and convince them to buy from you.

1

CREATE YOUR ONLINE IDENTITY

As the number of Americans on the Internet climbs toward the 200 million mark, online marketing has become one of the most successful and affordable ways to grow a small business. Soon, as many as a billion people will be connected globally, giving you access to a marketplace that's around the corner or around the world. Consumers and businesses use the Internet as a tool for daily communication via e-mail, plus as a key to the repository of the world's largest library. The Internet also provides an immediate liaison to entertainment. And it has entirely revolutionized where, when, and how we shop.

You'll find every type of consumer on the Internet—from children to seniors—and you can reach them on what may be the most level marketing playing field in existence. Any company, regardless of its size, can successfully master online marketing. So it makes sense that we start our 50 tips here.

When the Web was in its infancy, so much of the work to create a Web site and drive traffic there required some technical ability, or the deep pockets of larger companies that could afford to hire contracting firms to do the heavy lifting. But now, with the arrival of easy software programs that don't require any knowledge of HTML and low-cost services priced specifically for small businesses, you can create your own online marketing campaigns and find vendors to take a lot of the detailed high-tech work off your shoulders—without spending a fortune.

It all starts with your company Web site. Think of it as a static spot on the Web to which you must draw customers or clients. Your Web site exists quietly in cyberspace, and it takes a fair amount of "shouting" both online and off to get the word out. For that, you need an online marketing campaign, preferably one that dovetails with your off-line efforts.

If you operate an Internet-only business, you're part of a sweeping trend that has been gaining momentum and will continue to grow. Because Internet businesses can be founded virtually on a shoestring and operated from a home office full-time or part-time, they represent the emergence of a compelling low-cost start-up opportunity. Online retailers (e-tailers) can operate with little or no in-house inventory and free of the overhead of a brick-and-mortar store. The key is to consider your Web site a starting point and build an online marketing program to drive traffic. And as you grow, you can add additional off-line channels, such as direct mail.

Multichannel selling, through some combination of brick-and-mortar, catalogs, and online, results in increased sales. According to a 2004 Forrester Research report, the majority of all online consumers are cross-channel shoppers.[1] This is great news if you're a brick-and-mortar retailer and allow your customers the convenience of either shopping online or in your store. In fact, customers who shop through multiple channels spend as much as three times more than those who shop through one channel alone. What's more, customers who research specific products online but choose to make their purchases in the store have been shown to spend significantly more on additional products. This lucrative synergy accounts for the dramatic rise in small businesses whose customers and suppliers are within 50 miles of their location that now have Web sites and sell through multiple channels.

No matter whether you plan to sell exclusively online or through a combination of channels, it's essential to . . .

#1 PICK THE RIGHT DOMAIN NAME

If you sell off-line and have a recognized brand name or image, choosing a domain name is easy. Why would Toys "R" Us or Bed Bath & Beyond choose anything other than their store names as their URLs? Even companies without brick-and-mortar storefronts that have an established following can use what consumers remember best about their brands to create effective URLs. Consider the example of 1800flowers.com. After marketing this toll-free number extensively in off-line media, what may have been simply a memorable advertising call to action became a brilliant choice for a domain name.

For best results, the URL you choose should be either your company name or, better yet, what you market or what your site is all about. For example, the online home for Michigan-based American Blinds, Wallpaper & More is smartly named DecorateToday .com. Third-generation President Steve Katzman, who grew up in the family business, is a marketing whiz and the dynamic spokesperson you see in the company's television ads. The domain name encapsulates what his customers want to do and allows his company to move beyond the more confining product set of blinds and wallpaper to marketing everything from those core products to area rugs, bedding, framed art, lighting, and home accents.

If you're starting your business on the Internet or simply want to secure a URL that will resonate with customers, it's important to take into consideration the thinking process customers will go through when looking for what you market. A good domain name can help you show up in the right search engine results, and a memorable URL will stand out from the pack and build repeat visits. Suppose you were about to take your first skiing trip and were shopping for equipment. Your online search might turn up IfYouSki.com and you'd click through to the site because its domain name related specifically to what you were looking for.

Good domain names are easy to remember—such as PerfectPuppy .com, SitStay.com, and Find-A-Dog.com—but they're not always easy to come by. The most popular words and phrases are often in use or have been registered solely to *prevent* anyone from using them. When I registered our domain name, SmallBusinessNow .com, in 1998, I literally spent days submitting hundreds of word combinations before hitting on one that was not only available but would in some way convey what our site was all about. While there are numerous suffixes—including .net, .biz, .org, .info, and .us—.com is the one most commonly used by for-profit businesses. Therefore, it can make your site easier to find and remember if you register a domain name with a .com URL. Then you can register your chosen domain with additional suffixes, such as .net, just to be sure someone else doesn't register your same domain name with a different suffix and siphon off some of your traffic. If you operate a nonprofit, .org is appropriate for you.

You should also register your company and product names to protect them. Sony has a site called PlayStation.com, for example. Another strategy is to register sites with names your prospects may use when searching, just as Atari, for instance, has secured the site Games.com.

Registering multiple domains that contain keywords customers may use when searching can help your company achieve higher search engine rankings. But just because you have multiple domain names, you don't have to maintain content on numerous sites. Instead, you can use what's called "domain parking" and "point" multiple URLs at your primary Web site.

To begin your search for available domain names, visit a major Web-hosting company, such as Interland.com, SmallBusiness.Yahoo .com, or EarthLink.net, where you'll find forms that let you input your domain name requests and immediately find out whether or not they're available. And once you've found a domain name that meets your needs, you can register it for less than $10 a year.

The best Web-hosting companies will offer tools to help you create your site and track your traffic. But before you move forward, you'll need to decide exactly what kind of site you want to build.

There's an enormous benefit to marketing on the Web—it lets you dream big and act bigger. Unlike building a brick-and-mortar presence, there's no limit to the size or scope of your Web site. Small businesses running e-commerce sites list as many as 20,000 products. And small, nonprofit organizations have achieved national and international clout by virtue of a strong online presence.

The type of Web site you create will depend on your marketing goals. You can:

- Market a service locally, nationally, or internationally.
- Provide information through an e-zine, blog, or Web portal.
- Market a site related to a cause or issue.
- Create your own e-commerce site to sell products online.

You can create or build a brand online. On the Web, your site *is* your brand, and every interaction (or visit to your Web site) should equate to a positive branding experience. If you're like most small-business owners, you want your online marketing program to generate leads, build brand awareness and recognition, improve customer relationships, and even cross-sell and up-sell existing customers. Because an effective Web site is at the epicenter of all digital marketing efforts, you should follow certain important guidelines as you move forward and create your own unique site.

#2 SAVE WITH DO-IT-YOURSELF DESIGN

You may find the site creation tools provided by the major hosting companies sufficient for developing a basic site. For example, you can build a basic online store yourself with guidance from the software "wizards" provided by Yahoo! Small Business Merchant Solutions or from Interland. Some large hosting firms also offer custom Web design services to build deeper, more complex sites. However, custom site design, though much more affordable than in years past, still may be priced at several thousand dollars. So if you're looking for a lower-cost alternative, you can purchase software for about $200, such as Microsoft FrontPage, and save while creating your own, customizable Web design.

The design templates supplied by hosting companies and software makers will guide you step-by-step through the basics, but it's also important to know the design elements that make for the most effective sites. That way you can focus on the elements that are known to work best and steer clear of mistakes that can give your site an unprofessional look.

Eight Tips for Effective Web Design

For a site that's easy to navigate, loads quickly, and appears clean and uncluttered, just follow these eight design tips:

1. **Make navigation simple.** You can organize your site with navigation links in a toolbar down the left side, navigation buttons across the top, or both. What matters most is that your site is well organized and visitors can easily find what they're looking for. Follow the three-click rule: It should take no more than three clicks away from your main page to get to any product or service page on your site. If you have multiple target audiences, you can create separate sections of your site for each. For example, if you're targeting consumers as well as dealers or resellers, you can cleanly funnel traffic from each into separate sections of your site simply by structuring the navigation accordingly. And make each page of your site stand on its own, because you never know which page someone may choose to bookmark.

2. Design from the top down. For effective main page design, create a layout with the most critical elements closest to the top, starting with your logo and masthead (also known as a title graphic). Some visitors may look at your page very quickly and never scroll down beyond the first screen, so it's essential to display your most vital elements there. You can set special elements apart by using boxes or adding graphics and small photos.

3. Include a registration form. To conduct a successful online campaign, you'll need a database of customers who have "opted in" to receive your e-mail. So place a registration form near the top of your main page, and give visitors a good reason to sign up. (Learn more about this in Chapter 2.)

4. Consider your typeface. Don't try to squeeze too many elements in a small space. Always select type that's large enough to allow readers to comfortably scan your pages. For your Web pages to appear in the typeface you choose, your visitors must have it installed in their computers. So if you design in Tahoma but your visitors don't have Tahoma installed, then their default typeface will display, giving your site an entirely different look. To ensure your pages display properly, select the most common typefaces, such as Arial or Helvetica (both sans serif typefaces) or Times New Roman (a serif face). Serif faces are more traditional, while sans serif faces can appear more modern. Cursive fonts are attractive but may be difficult to read. Whichever typeface you choose, be sure to use it consistently. Designate one size font for all main headings and another for subheads throughout your site.

5. Choose colors carefully. The colors you choose for the principal elements on your site convey specific emotions to readers. We all know that blue is a cool color that's often associated with conservative businesses, while red, for example, is "hot" and indicates passion. How do you want your company to be perceived? And what colors resonate with your target audience? If you already have an established off-line company identity, you may choose to make minor alterations in your online color scheme if you believe your site will appeal to a somewhat different target group. Ordinarily, the best advice is to use color sparingly—that is, unless color is what your company is all about. That's the case for the unique Web site of Color Creek Fiber Art, http://www.color-creek .com, a company that specializes in dying fabric and clothing. Owner and artist, Mary Hertert, has created a site where vibrant color bursts from the borders of the page and helps to drive her company's message home.

6. Go for maximum readability. When it comes to making type readable, high contrast is the key. It's preferable to use dark text against a light background, and to stay away from busy or patterned backgrounds. Avoid putting text in all caps, which slows readers down and seems to "shout." Text should be aligned left and headlines work well when centered. Make all your links blue and avoid using other blue headings, which can easily be mistaken for live links.

7. Keep download time short. Web surfers are an impatient lot. It's best to keep your page download time to under 15 seconds, so beware of adding too much flash and animation, which can make your pages load slowly. Large photographs can also slow download time. Instead, use thumbnails that can be clicked on and enlarged. The way your photos look (grainy and rough versus sharp and clear) is a result of the image resolution and the type of file you use. GIFs are better suited for line art or flat colors, while JPEGs should be used for photos. Want to know which kinds of photos have the greatest impact? Images of attractive people looking directly at the viewer are proven to be the most engaging.

8. View your site in different Web browsers. Consistently carry your principal design elements throughout every page of your site, from your masthead design to the types of bullets, page colors, and typefaces you use. Then look at your site in all the common browsers your visitors might use. You'll be surprised to discover just how different your site looks from one to another. But most important, you'll be able to see if any design elements fail to display properly in all browsers, so that you can adjust them accordingly.

#3 CREATE COMPELLING ONLINE CONTENT

The only thing more important than your site's design is its content. A site with bare-bones design but terrific content will still be a hands-down winner. Increasingly, studies show that Internet users want more—that's *more* information in *less* time—and to prove it, overall page views are up while the amount of time spent per page is down. The number of sites visited in a single online session is on the rise, demonstrating that Web surfers are absorbing increasingly greater amounts of information and have less patience for sites that fail to meet their needs.

Why will people visit your site, and what will make them want to come back? Will you offer the best prices, the latest product reviews, hard-to-find items, a unique perspective on the news or an industry? Your answers will depend largely on the type of site you create, plus the way you differentiate your Web site from others with similar goals.

Superstores that sell on the Web, such as Target and Kohl's, offer an extensive range of products in dozens of categories. Small businesses that excel at e-commerce, on the other hand, tend to become recognized resources in one arena. They specialize in a wider selection in a particular category or group, and sell products that are a step up in price or quality or that can't be found elsewhere.

Suppose you're looking for a new backyard grill and you perform a basic online search for "barbecue grills." Chances are you'll turn up a site from Home Decor Products, Inc., http://www.barbecues .com, that's geared toward backyard entertaining. This site doesn't attempt to provide every kind of product under the sun, just what you might need to complete your outdoor barbecue experience— grills, smokers, outdoor furniture, lighting, and outdoor heaters (which you're probably going to need if you barbecue in the eve- nings). What the site provides is in-depth choices in its category with a long list of manufacturers' product lines from which to shop. In a highly contested product category, it's smart to be a specialist, just so long as your site offers a competitive advantage.

Even e-commerce sites that would otherwise compete solely based on price also must differentiate themselves. And you'll find one of most common methods is by providing in-depth content, including articles and product reviews.

Electronics, for example, remains one of the hottest online product categories. With literally tens of thousands of products and Web sites from superstores to specialists providing essentially the same items, creating a successful online electronics business may be the ultimate challenge. In an arena where parity products are available everywhere, offering the lowest price can be the de- ciding factor. But electronics shoppers are also voracious consum- ers of product information. They want to read more than what the manufacturer has to say—they demand reviews and feedback from customers about their purchases. In all, they want to get a feel for the "ownership experience," which is every bit as impor- tant as price for many shoppers. And their questions about the ownership experience aren't confined merely to the product and how it will perform. Like online shoppers in most product catego- ries, electronics shoppers also want to be certain the vendor they select will be dependable with regard to shipping and product re- turn policies.

For a stellar example of how to win at this game, small-business owners marketing electronics products can look to major online player CNET.com. The site provides a triple threat—reviews of thou- sands of products (just what you'd expect from a powerful publishing company), a sense of community (thanks to copious user reviews), and comparison shopping from what are termed "CNET certified" vendors. Like CNET, many smaller sites excel by offering the same type of well-rounded shopping experience. One such site, http://www.digitalcamerahq.com, includes a comprehensive listing of products, user and professional reviews, plus featured-merchant offers so visitors can select by price.

If you can't differentiate your site based on *what* you sell, try focusing on *how* you sell. For many service businesses, customer satisfaction is the bottom line. Site visitors want to know more than the general information about your company and what it delivers. That's where testimonials come in. They demonstrate to prospective customers or clients how well your company has performed for others in the past.

Testimonials are also useful to small-business owners who market their own products on their company Web sites, especially if these products are unique or not widely sold in stores. If you market private-label personal-care products, from cosmetics to bath salts, for instance, testimonials can relate your customers' personal experiences and how your proprietary products have met their needs. In fact, one of the best ways to reinforce *intangible* product benefits (such as looking good or feeling better) is by incorporating glowing testimonials from users into Web content and all your marketing materials.

Sometimes your Web content itself is your product. That's the case for Web portals and e-zines such as *DailyCandy*, an e-mail newsletter and Web site that puts an entertaining spin on "what's hot, new, and undiscovered—from fashion and style to gadgets and travel." Founded in 2000 by former print journalist Dany Levy, DailyCandy, Inc., was profitable by 2001, and in November of 2003 Levy partnered with the Pilot Group, a company started by MTV founder and AOL President Bob Pittman, which reportedly bought *DailyCandy* for between $3 and $4 million. Daily editions are available for key cities, including New York, Chicago, Los Angeles, Boston, and Dallas, as well as an "Everywhere," or national, issue. By early 2005, major advertisers that included Lancôme, American Express, Citibank, Paramount, and Bloomingdale's sponsored e-mails that reached 700,000 subscribers—all thanks to a unique approach to editorial content.

#4 MAKE E-COMMERCE PAY

Do you have an e-commerce Web site or plan to start one? One of the biggest challenges to online sales is the vast number of Internet users who research their purchases online but actually make them off-line in brick-and-mortar stores. In fact, consumers spend at least $1.70 off-line after online research for every dollar spent directly online, according to data from the 2004 Dieringer Research Group's "American Interactive Consumer Survey."[2] If you have a brick-and-mortar store as well as an e-commerce site, this may be good news—provided you can convince your online customers to make their purchases in *your* store.

Shoppers who buy off-line after conducting extensive research on the Internet often do so for immediate gratification. They can walk into a store and immediately walk out with their purchases without waiting for them to be shipped. Another reason comes down to indecision. Some shoppers want to compare numerous items and see them physically displayed in order to make a final choice. Others like to get an in-person look at certain types of products before buying. But an April 2005 Nielsen//NetRatings MegaView Online Retail report that ranked the top ten online sites based on sales conversions revealed a deeper story.[3] The bottom line is, while brick-and-mortar retailers with an online presence get more *shoppers*, it's the online-only retailers and catalogers (and one TV shopping network) that get more online *buyers*.

Yes, the Internet is a primary source of information for consumers when shopping for many types of products and services. Yet the number one job of an effective e-commerce site must be to convert shoppers into buyers.

Ten Ways to Close More Sales

To help you close more sales, here are ten ways to improve results from your e-commerce site:

1. **Build buyer confidence.** Customers want to know something about your company before they make a purchase. Include company information and background and, where appropriate, executive bios and photos, so customers know they're dealing with "real" people. Provide a "Contact Us" page with your company name, address, telephone number, and a form for e-mailing questions and comments.

2. **Excel at customer service.** Anticipate customer questions and provide a comprehensive Frequently Asked Questions page. In addition, online customer service can range from a bare-bones e-mail form for sending in questions to online customer service available in real time. The latter guarantees that the customer who's actively shopping on your site gets her questions answered immediately so that she can continue through the purchase process.

3. **Direct inbound traffic.** One way to increase online sales is to ensure that customers who click through to your site from your ads and promotions are directed to specialized landing pages. Instead of sending click-throughs to your main page, which forces customers to hunt through the rest of your site to take advantage of your offer, be sure customers are directed to specially designed pages where they can make a purchase with a minimum number of clicks.

4. **Make finding products easy.** A major complaint of many online shoppers is the difficulty they encounter when looking for specific products on comprehensive Web sites. Adding an on-site search facility can eliminate this problem and help customers find what they're looking for fast. This is of particular value to working

women who, studies show, are the most time-strapped consumers and cite "convenience" as a major reason for shopping online.

5. Provide multiple ways to order. Take your cue from successful DecorateToday.com and prominently display a toll-free number in the masthead of your site. That way, no matter what page of your site your customer is viewing she can immediately place an order or ask a question.

6. Make shoppers feel safe. From the customers' viewpoint, online security means much more than just using a secure connection when ordering. Customers also want to know that the private information they share with you will be kept safe and that they won't receive a barrage of spam as a result of shopping on your site. Post your company's privacy policy prominently, let customers know in what way their information will be used (such as whether you rent or share your customer list), and assure shoppers that their personal information will be secure with you.

7. Speed up the ordering process. You can speed up the checkout process for customers and dramatically reduce shopping cart abandonment by cutting down on the number of clicks (or pages a customer must view) to make a purchase. And give repeat customers preferential treatment that translates to speedy checkout. Although they may account for a relatively small percentage of your traffic, repeat customers have been shown to place items in a shopping cart as much as six times more frequently than customers who have not made a previous purchase.

8. Eliminate surprises at checkout. DoubleClick's "E-Commerce Site Trend Report" confirmed last year that nearly 60 percent of those who initially added something to their carts abandoned them without making a purchase.[4] You can help to eliminate this problem by making sure customers aren't surprised by high handling and shipping fees in the checkout process. Instead, provide a link for customers who want to learn about potential fees prior to checkout.

9. **Provide multiple payment options.** More payment options equate to increased sales. While the majority of online transactions are completed by credit card, you should offer as many as four payment options to your customers. This simple modification can increase your sales conversion rates by as much as 15 percent.

10. **Offer incentives at checkout.** Shipping costs may be the biggest hurdle for e-tailers. In fact, free or discounted shipping and handling often tops the list when consumers are asked to name their preferred purchase incentives. So if you can offer free shipping, a gift with purchase, or similar incentives at checkout, you can expect your online sales to climb as a result.

2

MARKET YOUR SITE

E-mail is a powerful, yet virtually free tool for cross-selling and up-selling current customers and drawing traffic to your site. Right now, customer retention has become the focus of most small-business e-mail campaigns because of the rising costs and diminished success of e-mail as a customer-acquisition tool. Can you guess the culprits? They're the dynamic duo—spam and pernicious viruses—clogging our mailboxes, threatening our ability to work and relax online safely, and making consumers everywhere tune out all but the most recognizable messages. Consumers generally define spam as unwanted e-mail from unknown sources, e-mail from a known source that comes too frequently, and e-mail with content that's irrelevant to their needs.

In years past, before most of us became inundated with the glut of spam, e-mail to rented, opt-in lists for the purpose of new customer acquisition performed well. But even though list rental costs have remained about the same, open rates and corresponding conversions from rented lists have diminished, making customer-acquisition campaigns using rental lists a costlier, higher-risk tactic.

The good news is that e-mail to an in-house database is a proven, low-cost way to generate leads and sales from current customers and prospects who have joined your company's proprietary list. This is called an "opt-in list" because individuals have elected the option of receiving information from your company by e-mail, and only permission-based lists should be used for your e-mail campaigns. When your subscribers (or list members) receive your e-mails, they know they're from a valued source of information and, as a result, are more likely to open and respond to them. Response rates from in-house, permission-based lists are typically at least as good as direct mail and often considerably better—without the cost of printing and postage.

#5 BUILD YOUR OWN OPT-IN LIST

Building a permission-based list is easy online. You can capture information from visitors who register on your site, and if you're an e-tailer you can acquire customer information and permission to send e-mails during the purchase process. Place a sign-up box or button on the main page of your site accompanied by brief copy that induces visitors to join your list. If building your list is a high priority, it's a good idea to place this sign-up option prominently on the page in a position where it will gain maximum attention. Create a simple, one-click button or single-entry form for your main page that clicks through to a more in-depth form. But don't go overboard. Make your registration form quick and easy to complete, such as by relying predominantly on checkboxes, and stay away from using longer forms, which actually discourage registration.

There are several effective ways to entice visitors to register. You can offer:

- A free newsletter
- Special notice of sales and new products
- Entry in a sweepstakes or contest

- • Access to members-only content
- • Participation in message boards or polls, or permission to post product reviews
- • Speedy online shopping and checkout for members

Though you'd never guess based on its 100,000-name e-mail list, Dance Distributors of Harrisburg, Pennsylvania, is a relative newcomer to online marketing. This dynamic small business was founded in 1940 by the grandfather of its current president, Mark Sussman, a savvy entrepreneur with an MBA in marketing. The move to online marketing in November of 2003 was a natural for the growing company, which launched its first print catalog in 1987, and today direct-mails 350,000 copies four times a year.

DanceDistributors.com calls itself "the dancer's source for value," and offers discounts on a range of brand-name products. Web site visitors who want to receive e-mails notifying them of sales and new products can click a sign-up button and be taken quickly to a simple form. Because Sussman's customers shop the site looking for value, it's a sure bet that the promise of even better prices on special offers will entice them to join his company's e-mail list.

Convincing Web site visitors to subscribe is essential to entrepreneur Michael Peterson, the founder of ShopCloseBuy.com, a neighborhood e-mail newsletter made up entirely of special promotions from local businesses in Minneapolis, St. Paul, and surrounding suburban neighborhoods. Back in 2002, Peterson had a strong desire to be his own boss. He was also living in an area experiencing strong urban renewal. He'd noticed that over a period of approximately five years about a hundred new places to wine, dine, and shop had moved into his neighborhood. But with all the new choices, he believed none of them really had done a good job of reaching out to him as a potential customer.

So Peterson took a week off from his job and set out to talk with 15 or so neighborhood business owners. When he found they had no easy way to market to the local target audience, he came up with the idea of an advertiser-supported promotional e-mail. Fortunately, 14 of the 15 business owners Peterson talked to thought the promotional e-mail would be good for the neighborhood—and what's more, they said they'd be willing to pay to advertise in it. That's when Peterson decided to start his own business. As of March of 2005, his subscriber list had reached 20,000 and 50 merchants were participating advertisers. In addition, his company now creates newsletters for individual merchants.

What entices visitors to sign up on the ShopCloseBuy.com Web site? "Freebies, discounts, and special offers from shops, restaurants, and service providers" and a promise that "each e-mail features special promotions from local businesses in your areas of interest." Neighborhood residents subscribe because they want to know where and how to find the best local deals. Wouldn't you?

Because convenience and easy shopping are vital to online customers, particularly working women who are major online consumers, many shoppers are willing to preregister to secure speedy service and checkout. Visitors to DecorateToday.com, for example, can register to speed their online shopping by gaining access to their shopping carts from any computer they choose and eliminating the need to reenter their personal information each time they visit the online store.

You can build your e-mail list using off-line tactics, too. Capturing e-mail addresses and other customer information at checkout is a common practice among brick-and-mortar retailers. The ShopCloseBuy.com merchants, for instance, actively recruit subscribers. Participating businesses take the old-fashioned fishbowl approach. Peterson has created signage that reads "Drop in your business card for a chance to win [some kind of prize] and you'll also receive an e-mail with special offers from this store and other neighborhood shops." As a result, Peterson gains permission to send two types of e-mail: one from ShopCloseBuy.com and another exclusively from individual merchants.

Customers who shop off-line via direct mail or telephone from Dance Distributors can also be added to the company's permission-based e-mail list. Here's how: When a customer calls in a phone order, she's asked whether she would care to receive information online. The salesperson then includes the caller's e-mail address in the customer record and the customer is automatically added to the DanceDistributors.com opt-in list.

No matter whether you gather your permission-based list information exclusively online, by direct mail, through telephone contact, or in person, you'll need an efficient way to manage and make smart use of the information you gather. That's why it's essential to . . .

#6 SET UP AN IN-HOUSE DATABASE

The database you create should include any and all information that will be helpful to building your business. E-mail addresses are only part of the equation. When you capture registrations on your Web site, it's a great idea to gather information that will help you understand your customers—who they are and what they need— so you can tailor your product and service offers accordingly.

If you were to look at the online registration forms of the companies you've been reading about, here's what you'd find:

- DanceDistributors.com requires only first name, last name, e-mail address, and a password, but it also requests demographics, including the registrant's birth date, gender, and ZIP code. To further help the company understand its customers and create messages that will meet their needs, DanceDistributors.com asks customers to check off all the descriptions that apply to them: dance teacher, dancer, studio owner, parent, store owner, or nondancer. The final question asks registrants to simply click on their areas of interest—ballet, jazz, cheer, or children's wear, among other options.
- ShopCloseBuy.com asks new subscribers to supply their ZIP codes when registering. This is primarily to help the mer-

chants who advertise in the promotional e-mail newsletter to pinpoint exactly where their customers are coming from. After inputting a ZIP code, new registrants click through to a form that allows them to select the neighborhood newsletters and types of promotions and offers they'd like to receive. All this information is added to the ShopCloseBuy.com subscriber database.

- The online newsletter *DailyCandy* uses a quick subscription form comprised predominantly of checkboxes. (Remember, it's essential to keep your form simple and easy.) Subscribers select a *DailyCandy* edition, whether they want their version in HTML or plain text, type in their names, select their country, and ZIP code. In addition, new subscribers are asked the kind of basic demographic information that the company's national advertisers no doubt require, including age, gender, and income. The ability to analyze the database based on demographics can have significant benefits when shaping editorial content as well.

Maintaining a comprehensive, in-house database containing customer records doesn't have to cost a fortune. Low-cost software is available, including GoldMine 6.5 by FrontRange, that helps you track all sales and marketing activities as well as maintain vital demographic and sales information. These off-the-shelf software products should serve your small business well until the size of your company or database requires you to seek custom solutions.

What's the difference between constructing and maintaining a complete customer database and simply assembling an e-mail list? Formulating a permission-based e-mail list will let you send e-mail to customers and prospects. But acquiring additional data will tell you almost everything you need to know about *what* to send them. You can segment your list based on areas of interest or other factors and then e-mail only the most relevant content and offers. This can dramatically increase your response rates, generate more sales, and take you one step closer to building positive customer relations.

#7 MAXIMIZE CUSTOMER RETENTION WITH E-MAIL

For e-mail to work as a customer retention tool, it's essential to measure customer response and fine-tune your program over time. You can test different elements individually by varying components in your mailings. For example, you can routinely try out new subject lines, offers, and article content until you achieve superior results. Just be sure to test one element at a time, so it's clear exactly which lead to incremental improvement.

Ten Basic Elements of an E-mail Campaign

You can easily manage your own e-mail campaign, which starts with an understanding of these ten basic elements:

1. **Bounces.** These are e-mails that are sent but not delivered because of a bad address, the recipient's mailbox is full, or they are blocked as spam. Individual e-mail filters and spam blockers as well as spam protection offered by Internet service providers (ISPs) often mistake legitimate e-mails, particularly newsletters and solicitations, for spam. This problem can be reduced by using a reputable e-mail marketing service.

2. **Open rate.** The number of recipients who receive your e-mail but decide not to open it can make or break your campaign. Because average open rates vary by industry and type of mailing (though a number somewhere between 35 percent and 40 percent is often cited), it's impossible to tell you what you should expect your open rate to be. However, enough customers and prospects must open your e-mail and take action in order for your campaign to achieve its goals. And only you can decide whether a satisfactory open rate is 25 percent, 50 percent, or more.

3. "From" line. The majority of e-mail recipients scrutinize the name of the sender when deciding whether or not to open an e-mail. Be certain that your e-mails are immediately recognizable as coming from you, a valued source of information.

4. Subject line. Like the "from" line, the subject line can instantly persuade your recipients to open your e-mail or discard it. Anything that smacks of spam will be rejected. Avoid personal greetings, such as "How are you?" which virtually scream spam. Instead, take time to carefully craft a subject line that includes a benefit or, at the very least, lets the recipient clearly know what your e-mail is about. Studies show that short subject lines perform best because they can be viewed in their entirety by recipients who are making quick decisions about whether to open your e-mail. So to achieve a higher open rate, keep your subject line to just four or five words.

5. Hyperlinks. The goal of an e-mail campaign is to get the recipients to do something. While your e-mail itself should contain all the information readers need to make a decision to move forward, ultimately they'll have to click on a link to make a purchase or learn more. Studies show that keeping hyperlinks plentiful can increase results, as can placing them throughout your text so readers don't have to scroll through all your copy to take action.

6. Click-through rate. This is the number of recipients who click on a link in your e-mail to take advantage of an offer or get more information. If you have a high open rate but low click-through, it's an indication that your content failed to motivate readers.

7. Conversion rate. This represents the number of click-throughs that convert to sales. If you're marketing a product or service and have a high click-through rate with few sales, your e-mail may not be at fault. Instead, the landing page, Web site, or checkout process may be the culprit.

8. Opt-out option. The CAN-SPAM Act of 2003 mandated that e-mails must contain your company name and postal address as well as an opt-out mechanism. So make sure all e-mails to your list include an easy unsubscribe option. Most mailers include this at the bottom of every e-mail along with a privacy notice explaining how customer data is used. When someone chooses to unsubscribe, they should receive an auto response confirming that his or her address has been removed.

9. Frequency. The timing of your e-mail is more important than you might imagine. Because e-mail that arrives too frequently may be considered spam, it's important to gauge how often to contact your list. You don't want to abuse the permission customers have given you to contact them by e-mail. Varying the types of e-mail you send, such as by alternating newsletters with solicitations, is considered an acceptable way to achieve higher frequency without burning out your list. You'll need to monitor customer feedback and examine the rise or fall of your open rate to determine if you're contacting customers too often.

10. Content. If your content's not relevant, readers will tune you out and your open rate will plummet. So put yourself in your customers' or clients' shoes and decide exactly what they would most like to receive from you.

One of the biggest boons to small businesses has been the arrival of e-mail marketing services priced so affordably it hardly pays to do it yourself. At this writing, the e-mail marketing services that assist small businesses charge a monthly fee based on the number of subscribers on your list, and most will e-mail up to 5,000 subscribers, for example, for $50 a month or less. Several e-mail marketing services cater to small businesses, but the one I've thoroughly tested is Constant Contact. The company describes what it offers as "Do-it-yourself e-mail marketing," and I've found that Constant Contact can perform a lot of the tedious, time-consuming work while allowing you to oversee and effectively manage your e-mail campaigns.

When choosing an e-mail marketing service, look for one that provides design templates for newsletters, promotional offers, coupons, and invitations. It's helpful if these designs not only look great, but are also easy to customize. The e-mail marketing service should maintain and clean your list by removing bounces and the addresses of people who choose to unsubscribe, and deliver the e-mails on the schedule you designate, no matter how large or small your list. It's also very important that the service provides all the campaign metrics, so you can see how effective your e-mail campaigns are—including who opened your e-mail and clicked on each link—and compare your results from one mailing to the next.

Without an e-mail marketing service, it's difficult for a small-business owner to send more than 50 e-mails at a time, because higher numbers are usually blocked as spam by ISPs. So if you have a list of just several hundred subscribers, you may be comfortable breaking it down into groups of 50 and sending it out. But as your list grows, you'll want to look for a vendor, especially to take advantage of all the reports provided.

#8 CREATE A COMPANY E-NEWSLETTER

E-newsletters are a terrific way to communicate with customers or clients and prospects without taking a hard-sell approach. Traditionally, newsletters have been editorial in nature, though some e-tailers have begun to call what would normally be thought of as solicitations (including sales promotions) newsletters. Softer-sell, editorially focused newsletters are ideal communications tools for service businesses, from financial planning firms to landscape design companies, and manufacturers of everything from software to skateboards. You can share information with customers, position your company or yourself as expert in your field, receive useful feedback, introduce new products and services, increase traffic to your Web site, and, ultimately, build stronger customer relationships.

Basically, two types of e-newsletter editorial styles are used: short blurbs with links to longer articles, or one major article interspersed with ads or promotional links. Some members of your list who are using dial-up connections may prefer to receive their newsletters in plain text only, while many others, especially those with broadband, will be accustomed to receiving newsletters in HTML, complete with photos and graphics. You may choose to create a text-only newsletter, which your entire list will be able to download quickly and view, but your e-mail will have little or no visual punch, and recipients who are accustomed to HTML newsletters may find yours somewhat antiquated in appearance. A better choice is to design a full-color, high-impact HTML newsletter using a template provided by an e-mail marketing service or affordable software, such as FrontPage, and give recipients the option of receiving a text-only version.

The key to success is to make your content so compelling that customers and prospects will look forward to receiving your e-newsletter. What type of stories, articles, or information will your audience find most appealing? Will your e-newsletter contain industry or technology news, how-to articles, entertaining items and trends, or commentary on events? Decide on the theme for your newsletter and then give it an appropriate name. The name you choose to appear on the masthead of your e-newsletter should communicate something to the subscriber, just as the name of a major magazine (whether *Entrepreneur* or *Vogue*) proudly indicates to the reader, "This is for you."

For positive results, keep your design, tone, and format consistent from one issue to the next. Carry your company's off-line identity into your online marketing by including your company logo along with the newsletter name in the masthead. Much as your company brochure incorporates such essential design elements, your e-newsletter should also have a look that's unique to your business.

The best way to use an e-newsletter to enhance your image or build a brand is by repeating key elements, from design components through company messages, in every issue over time. This will go a long way toward helping to warm up cold prospects, moving them incrementally along in your sales cycle by instilling customer confidence in your small business. It's also smart to send your newsletter on a regular schedule to reinforce this positive image of dependability.

Customers appreciate articles that simplify complex topics. For example, a newsletter can help you relate how to get the most from financial products, provide health care how-tos, or explain industry regulations and the ways your readers can meet them. Customers also enjoy case histories because they show how others like themselves have found solutions to challenges. And case histories demonstrate your abilities without overt selling. It's imperative you keep your company news to a minimum. The focus of your e-newsletter must be on "you," the customer, not "us," the company.

If you choose to build the editorial content of each issue around one long article, make it no more than 500 to 1,000 words, because longer pieces may discourage readers. Include numerous links to your site and provide readers with good reasons to click through. Many e-newsletters invite readers to send comments, which is a terrific way to encourage a dialogue between you and your customers or clients and prospects.

Want to increase the size of your subscriber list? Try adding a "forward e-mail" or "send to a friend" option to your e-newsletter. This is used to great advantage by the e-newsletter, *DailyCandy*. Its founder, Dany Levy, asserts, "We grow 500 to 1,000 new subscribers a day basically by people hitting the forward button."

If you'd rather spend your time running your business than writing your newsletter, don't despair. You don't have to create all your own newsletter content. You can get help from expert contributors. Authors promoting new books, for example, will sometimes waive their writer's fee or permit a book excerpt to be published. You can also approach freelance writers to create individual articles. When searching for freelancers, look at Web sites that contain subject matter similar to yours and contact the writers who have experience creating articles such as the ones you'd like to publish. That way you won't pay for their "learning curve," and your cost will be considerably lower. Another option is to hire a professional copywriter to create all your newsletter copy.

Here are your choices ranked by potential cost:

- Your no-cost option is to assemble an e-newsletter comprised of short blurbs from different authors and sources that you obtain in exchange for attribution or promotion. Just be sure the body copy of each piece resides on *your* Web site, so all the click-throughs go to you.
- The second option is to purchase one principal piece from a qualified freelancer and make that the focus of each issue. You should be prepared to offer payment for services rendered. The fee will depend on the writer and the length of the piece.
- The third possibility, which is the one with the highest direct cost, is to contract with a copywriter to create the content for your newsletter in its entirety. You may be able to negotiate a more favorable rate by contracting for multiple issues.

#9 SEND LOW-COST E-MAIL PROMOTIONS

Ask small-business owners from coast-to-coast and they'll tell you their top reasons for choosing promotional e-mail over other forms of marketing are its low cost, speedy delivery, and customer response, and the ability to easily measure return on investment (ROI). Add to that the capacity to target a large audience with a single campaign, plus easy implementation—even with personalized messaging—and it's plain to see why e-mail promotions are becoming popular tools among marketers nationwide.

The bottom line is that promotions to permission-based lists are generally well received, even welcomed. Nearly one-third of respondents to DoubleClick's consumer e-mail study said they had made an immediate online purchase as the result of receiving a permission-based e-mail, and close to one-third said they had clicked on messages for information and later made an online purchase as a result.[1] This is a perfect example of the responses you can expect to receive from a combination of click-through and longer-term postimpression activity, called "view-through."

You can send e-mail with sales promotions, coupons, customer reward information, invitations to events—just so long as what you send is of special interest to your audience. Mark Sussman of Dance Distributors says one successful e-mail promotion that definitely increased sales for his company offered a free Capezio shoe bag with the purchase of any Capezio shoes. Dance Distributors uses a Web developer, Pipeline Interactive, that maintains the Web site and provides e-mail software for a monthly fee, so Sussman's team can easily create and send out their own e-mail promotions. With 300 bags to give away and a list of approximately 100,000, the campaign's open rate was 30 percent, with click-through over 5 percent. Thanks to a speedy, positive response, Sussman says they had to stop the promotion quickly because all 300 bags were given away to happy purchasers.

If you're an e-tailer, in addition to new promotions you should also consider sending e-mail to customers immediately following purchases. Many consumers indicate they're receptive to promotional e-mail following e-commerce purchases, making promotion of ancillary offers by e-mail a strong tactic. For example, more than half the respondents to DoubleClick's study said they'd be interested in offers for related products, and nearly half expressed interest in receiving information about membership reward programs.

But you don't have to be an e-tailer to enjoy great success with e-mail promotions. Small businesses marketing consumer services can use e-mail promotions instead of direct mail to reach large customer and prospect databases for virtually no cost. Business-to-business marketers can segment their e-mail lists by type of business or other criteria and then send different e-mail promotions to each group. This will ensure that the targeted recipients always receive information tailored to their distinct interests.

For example, Tulsa, Oklahoma–based Media Specialists, Inc., markets quality audiotape and videotape and equipment. Its high-energy, dynamic president is Corinne Dalby, who has made personalized service and attention to detail her company's mission. And it's this commitment to excellence that has enabled her to build her business year after year since 1998. Dalby's database of more than 1,000 customers and prospects is managed using ACT!, contact and customer management software, and is segmented based on the types of businesses her company serves, including broadcast media and production companies, large ministries, general corporate purchasers, government agencies, and schools. Because the media and equipment needs of a television station vary significantly from those of a large church, for instance, Dalby creates separate e-mails for each segment of her database. They may feature Sony cameras and other equipment or special pricing on videotape. E-mails are personalized for every recipient and the messages are written so they are extremely relevant to the needs of each targeted group.

For some types of service businesses, taking a softer approach to e-mail promotions works best. This has certainly proven to be the case for Jeff Porro, PhD, the principal of Porro Associates, a Washington, D.C.–area firm. A highly skilled communicator, Porro writes op-eds, speeches, and press material for PR firms, nonprofits, and other corporate clients, and it's not uncommon for his op-eds to appear in some of the nation's most prominent newspapers. When an op-ed he wrote for a client ran in the *Chicago Sun-Times,* Porro decided to demonstrate to his e-mail database the kind of high-quality work he could produce.

With the goal of stimulating appointments to discuss potential projects, Porro sent the op-ed text to his list of 80 prospects and clients. He began each e-mail with a very simple personal note saying he thought they might be interested in his latest op-ed. And while a list of 80 people may seem small to you, it's actually quite comprehensive when you consider the specialized nature of Porro's work. The list is maintained in Outlook and is composed of three segments: lobbyists, grass-roots firms, and a mix of PR firms and nonprofit groups. This list has also received Porro's ongoing off-line promotion that includes postcards and dimensional mail (more about his success with this in Chapter 6).

Want to know the results of Porro's quick and easy e-mail promotion? In the first day, he received two immediate appointments and a reply from another prospect who asked to schedule an appointment a month later. Overall, there were 9 positive responses within 24 hours. There was even one important prospect who responded, "YOU ROCK. I have your candle and stress-management kit on my desk [*this refers to the dimensional mail kit Porro sent months earlier*]. Let me think about how we can use you in April, May." Porro's marketing program is a terrific example of how an ongoing campaign that combines smart, effective online and off-line promotion can motivate prospects and win sales.

Tips for Writing Promotional E-mail

When it comes to creating your own e-mail promotions, you can use a design template from an e-mail marketing service or software program, or, like Porro, you can send a text-only e-mail, which tends to make a more personal, softer-sell appeal. And for many types of businesses it's the appropriate way to communicate. Here are nine important tips for writing promotional e-mail content:

1. **Communicate one-to-one.** Recipients read your e-mails as individuals not as a group. Use the same tone you would when writing a letter to a friend or business associate.

2. Personalize your e-mail. For best results, it's a good idea to start your e-mail by addressing the reader by name. Remember, it's important to gather this information when prospects register or subscribe to receive your e-mail.

3. Keep it concise. The optimal length for a text-only e-mail is about 250 words. Keep paragraphs short, just three or four sentences at most.

4. Use a strong hook. The first two sentences of your e-mail are the most critical. They contain your hook, or special offer, and they have to grab the readers and compel them to continue.

5. Maintain excitement through the body copy. In the body of your e-mail, explain how readers will receive the benefits promised in your hook. Intersperse links throughout to stimulate response.

6. Have a call to action. Close your e-mail with a strong reason for readers to click through. Be specific, and state precisely what recipients should do next.

7. Include a signature. For many types of e-mail promotions, a personal appeal from you, the president of your small business, is essential. At the end of this type of e-mail, be certain to include your signature block and professional title. No matter whether you have one employee (yourself) or 100, you're still the president

8. End with a postscript. Just like in direct-mail marketing, you can include a postscript at the end of your promotional e-mail to restate your hook or offer. Readers who barely skim the body copy may check out your P.S. when deciding whether or not to spend time with your e-mail.

9. Provide multiple contact options. It's always a good idea to supply a toll-free telephone number as well as online links and an e-mail address through which customers can respond. Giving customers more than one way to contact you can help to increase your response rate.

Effective e-mail marketing will drive traffic to your site, stimulate customer response, and increase product and service sales. This is one of the lowest-cost ways to market a growing business—and it's a marketing tactic no small business can afford to overlook.

3

BUILD AN
ONLINE PROGRAM

If you're looking for a way to generate leads and find new customers—and you want to make every dollar count—you need a comprehensive online campaign. The Web makes it possible to conduct a complete advertising and public relations program for a fraction of the cost of a comparable off-line campaign. This is where the utility of the Web as a level playing field really excels.

The secret to maximizing your online savings is to pinpoint your narrowest possible target group. In fact, narrowly defining the profile of your online prospects will actually save you money because you won't need to scatter your ads across a wide range of sites or advertise on the main pages of the large megasites that reach general audiences. Instead, you'll place your message only where it's virtually guaranteed to find the right audience, often on smaller sites or specific, content-rich Web pages.

#10 TARGET YOUR BEST PROSPECTS

You'll find you can afford a surprisingly deep, comprehensive campaign provided you focus exclusively on your best prospects. These are qualified individuals who have demonstrated a predisposition to buy what you sell. Before you can create a successful online campaign, you must understand these potential customers and how they use the Internet.

Start by writing a one-paragraph description of your target audience. If you're marketing to consumers, you'll create a target audience profile. This is a brief but detailed description of your prospects based on demographics, including age, gender, and any other characteristics that may qualify them, such as their household incomes, educational backgrounds, where they live, or if they have children in a certain age group.

Suppose you sell Spanish-language music CDs. Here's an example of a simple target audience profile you might create:

> Latino men who reside in the United States, ages 18 to 24, with a demonstrated interest in music and entertainment products, household incomes $18,000 plus, and who possess a major credit card.

If you're a business-to-business marketer, instead of a target audience profile, you'll need a simple description of your best prospects broken down by category or SIC code plus all their qualifying characteristics. For example:

> Chief information officers with responsibility for quality-control software in small to midsize manufacturing companies with 250 to 500 employees and a minimum of 20 computer workstations, in XYZ SIC codes.

Once you've profiled your best prospects, you'll need to determine why they use the Internet and what types of sites they frequent. As you'll discover, every target group has somewhat different Internet usage patterns. A study from Nielsen//NetRatings and WashingtonPost.com in 2004 found that working women, for example, rely on the Web predominantly for shopping and product research.[1] And according to a 2005 BIGresearch survey, Latinos research apparel online more than any other category, while African-Americans research shoes.[2]

With a little bit of digging, you can discover what your prospects typically accomplish on the Internet and the types of sites they visit. Based on this knowledge, you can choose a combination of online marketing tactics—from paid search and other forms of advertising to PR and creating your own blog—all designed to touch your best prospects at critical points in the buying process. And you can create an effective online marketing program to generate leads and sales, establish your company or brand image, and drive traffic to your Web site.

#11 MASTER PAID SEARCH

Nearly 85 percent of Internet users perform online searches, according to the Pew Internet & American Life Project report.[3] How will they find you?

Of the two types of search, paid and organic, paid search is the way to guarantee your message reaches prospects who are actively looking to buy what you sell. Customers use online search engines at a crucial point in the purchase process—when they have an idea of what they want and are looking for the right place to buy it. Unlike organic (or natural) search rankings, buying paid search advertising guarantees your ad will appear near the top—or at least in the first page or two—of search results where it's most likely to gain attention, not many pages down. In fact, some recent studies have shown that only the top results are viewed by the majority of searchers. And one study concluded that sites that appear on the first page of results may attract six times the traffic and double the sales. You can optimize your site so that it performs better in organic listings (more about this next), but if you want to ensure that your Web site gets sufficient traffic to build sales, you'll need a combination of high-ranking paid listings as well as organic ones.

The principle behind paid search is simple. You bid on keywords or keyword phrases and pay when someone clicks on your ad. Although prices vary, there's no need to buy the most expensive keywords. At this writing, the average cost per click is under $0.50.

Every major search engine offers some form of paid listings, from Google (the most popular and often-used engine) and Yahoo! through MSN and AOL, and they are engaged in something of a turf war for their slice of this very big pie. But there's no need for you to take sides. The majority of Internet searchers use multiple search engines, and it's a smart idea for search marketers to use three or four search engines and buy dozens (even hundreds) of keywords or keyword pairs per month.

Here's how it works:

- Your first step is to identify the keywords (really keyword phrases) your prospects search on to find what you market.
- Then you bid on them and set a ceiling based on how many clicks you're willing to pay for per month. Advertisers who bid the highest get the best placements.
- Next, you'll need to create ads to run on the results pages. Depending on the search engine, these may run across the top of the search results or down the right side, and they may appear in boxes or strictly as text with links.
- The wording of your ads is crucial to the success of your paid search campaign, so fine-tune the copy until it yields maximum results.
- Send click-throughs to specialized landing pages where customers can immediately take advantage of your offer.
- Continuously monitor your results carefully, including which keywords yield the greatest click-through and your conversion rate per click-through for each ad.

If you think this sounds like a lot of work, an alternative that's bound to save you time and money is to turn to a search engine marketing (SEM) service. This is one low-cost option that shouldn't be overlooked.

Just ask Mary Hertert, a talented artist and owner of Color Creek Fiber Art in Anchorage, Alaska. Through her Web site, http://www.color-creek.com, Hertert offers fabric dyeing and dyed fabric art. Hertert uses an SEM service called MyEZClicks, provided through her Web-hosting company, Interland, and pays less than $50 a month for paid listings on a comprehensive list of search engines using 21 keywords and keyword pairs, including "custom dyeing" and "art textiles," for example. The service is completely turnkey and guaranteed, so Hertert doesn't have to be an expert in writing ad copy or devote hours to running her campaign, and she can easily monitor the program and evaluate her conversion results.

Her eight-year-old small business has flourished as a result of this affordable campaign, and Hertert is delighted to say that she did more custom dyeing work in the first six months of her paid search program than she did in the previous five years. "Before paid search, no one could find me," says Hertert. What's more, this program has allowed her to transform the nature of the work her company performs. In 1997, just 4 percent of the company's revenues were from commercial dyeing, which now accounts for 55 percent of its business.

Paid search can also be used to launch a fledgling business that might otherwise be virtually "invisible." When Patti Pavel's dog, Alex, suffered from terrible indigestion, she researched natural food options and soon discovered holistic pet food—and a new career as a distributor. Her one-year-old company, The Healthy Holistic Pet, is an Internet reseller of Flint River Ranch pet food, http://www.frrholisticpet.com.

To get her new online business off the ground, Pavel jumped into paid search. Using Google and Overture (now Yahoo! Search Marketing), the first weekend she ran her campaign, Pavel got

$500 in sales. The trouble was it cost her $250. Although she was convinced of the power of paid search, she needed a more afford-able solution, and now uses the same low-cost SEM service as Hertert. Before she started advertising, Pavel had 10 customers, today she has 200, and paid search drives 50 percent of her traffic. In 2005, Pavel planned a move from Rochester Hills, Michigan, to North Carolina, added new products, and set a goal of $20,000 in sales from her site.

Of course, national and international search opportunities miss the mark for many types of local businesses that draw their customers or clients from their local areas. The great news is that local online ads appear to persuade shoppers. According to a 2005 study by Dieringer Research Group, Inc., local online shoppers reported that the Internet influenced at least 7 purchase decisions in the fourth quarter of 2004, while newspapers were an influential factor for just 3.5 purchases and local TV affected only 2 buying decisions.[4]

Plumbing companies, restaurants, spas, antiques shops, fine jewelers—just about any kind of local business you can name—can benefit from local paid search listings. This is the hottest new form of search available, and you'll find many companies competing for your paid search dollars, including online Yellow Pages directories.

Off-line, the print Yellow Pages consume a huge percentage of local advertisers' budgets. You may choose to reduce your financial outlay by moving a portion of your off-line Yellow Pages expenditures online, which represents a lower-cost opportunity to try a proven customer acquisition method. But don't do so at the expense of the major search engines, particularly Google. By 2009, strategic research and analysis provider The Kelsey Group predicts the local search market will have grown to $3.4 billion, outpacing Internet Yellow Pages, which the group puts at a $1.3 billion industry.[5]

Although the local search offerings vary from one search engine to another, essentially you have the ability to place ads within a state, city, or metropolitan area, or even choose a radius from a given point—from half a mile to 100 miles. Google Local Search includes Google maps, user reviews, hours of operation, and credit cards accepted. Its closest competitor, Yahoo!, also offers integrated advanced mapping and user reviews in its local product, and AOL's search site, Local.aol.com, brings together a collection of local content to make its search results comprehensive. Best of all, you won't have to compete for high-cost terms (keyword phrases) and can limit your spending to locally targeted customers. This will enable you to purchase more valuable terms at a lower total cost.

But what if you market brand-name products, such as cameras or computer software programs, and want to reach a well-qualified, national audience at the lowest possible cost? Your best choice may be paid search on "vertical" shopping sites, where serious shoppers turn when they want to compare prices and vendors. You can place pay-per-click ads on general shopping sites, such as Yahoo! Shopping, where ads are priced by category. And you can secure merchant or product listings on highly specific sites that include product reviews, such as CNET.com, which is dedicated exclusively to technology products. Sites that provide reviews and other substantial content draw information-seeking shoppers who enjoy the convenience of researching and comparing products, then making their purchases all on one comprehensive site. Customers who might otherwise be reluctant to buy products from an unknown seller are comfortable placing their orders on sites where they know the vendors have been screened and admitted to a listing program or have been reviewed by previous purchasers.

#12 OPTIMIZE YOUR SITE

The flip side of paid search is search engine optimization (SEO). Like paid search, the ultimate goal is to have your site turn up near the top of search results. And you can optimize your own site to improve organic search results with zero financial outlay.

Optimization can boost your site traffic considerably. In fact, in a Search Marketing Survey of approximately 3,000 marketers by MarketingSherpa.com, they said organic clicks increased an average of 73 percent in the six months after optimization.[6]

Six Steps to Improve Your Organic Search Rankings

Here are six steps you can take to raise your company's organic rankings:

1. **Increase inbound links.** The best "ranked" sites are the ones that list highest in organic search results. This ranking is based primarily on the number of prominent sites that link to yours and how well the content of your pages matches the keywords used in the search. The more links you can acquire *to* your site from high-ranking referrers, the better your chances of appearing near the top of search results. Google, for example, uses an algorithm that puts high emphasis on link popularity. Sometimes, obtaining links from just a handful of major sites, such as prominent industry associations or Web portals, can raise your rankings. On the other hand, you might need links to your site from thousands of small sites to achieve the same result. To successfully optimize your site, contact relevant referrers and offer to exchange links, and set up links from all related industry sites and Web portals.

2. **Make your content keyword rich.** Which keyword phrases are your targeted prospects most likely to search for? If you're unsure, you can always check your competition for ideas. Perform searches using keyword phrases that you know you want to use and click through to the top sites that come up. For even more ideas, you can look at the keywords your competitors have in their meta tags (the HTML coded tags the search engines read) by clicking on "View" at the top of your Web browser and then selecting "Page Source" to look through the HTML code.

Avoid general keywords, because too much competition will be standing in your way of a high rank. The traffic you get will be much better qualified if you choose more specific phrases. For example, instead of a general keyword such as "fishing," you'll have better success if you optimize for the keyword phrase "fiberglass fishing rods." And there's no need to limit yourself to a short list. You can use as many keyword phrases as necessary when optimizing your pages.

Sprinkle your keyword phrases throughout your site. Use them in the text on every page, in text hyperlinks, the title tag on each page, and in photo labels (alt tags).

3. Create a great title tag. The title tags are critical to successful optimization because they're what the search engines generally use as the titles of your listings in search results. If you're working in a software program, such as FrontPage, it's easy to customize your page properties and add the appropriate copy—without having to learn any HTML programming. Make your title tag between 50 and 80 characters long, with spaces, and include your most important keyword phrase. Above all, it's essential you make your title compelling because it has to induce searchers to click through to your site.

4. Optimize the "description" and "keywords" meta tags. While you're customizing your page properties, be sure to create "description" and "keywords" meta tags. Include several of your most important keyword phrases in your description meta tag. Limit it to about 250 characters, and describe your page content in a way that will entice visitors to click through. When writing your keywords meta tag, it's important to use only keyword phrases that appear on that Web page, including those within your other tags. And you can list plural versions, such as "fiberglass fishing rod" and "fiberglass fishing rods."

You can also place keyword phrases in text hyperlinks to achieve higher rankings. And you can customize image (alt) tags as well, by including an important keyword phrase in the description that relates to each image. Here's an example that describes a photo of a man fishing at sunset: "Great results with a fiberglass fishing rod in Key West, Florida."

5. Help local searchers. If you're targeting local traffic, you can optimize your site by adding local search terms to your tags, like the one previously mentioned. For example, your title tag might be "Fiberglass Fishing Rods, Key West, Florida." In addition, sprinkle local search terms throughout all your Web pages.

6. Be patient. You can either submit your site for review to individual search engines, or you can sit back and wait for their "spiders" to find you. Monthly submission is often ideal at the outset, so if you choose to be proactive, you may want to use an economical service such as Microsoft's Submit It! or Submit Express to submit your site information for you. The cost is usually less than $100 and the service eliminates all the detailed work of filling out each search engine's forms, usually by creating a single form and submitting it for you automatically. The service will also send you reports on which engines are listing your pages in organic searches.

Once you've optimized your site, you may be anxious to see how well it performs in searches. But don't be surprised if it takes six weeks or more for your hard work to pay off—even if you rely on a submission service. It takes a minimum of four weeks to get organic listings on Google, six weeks on Excite, and up to two months on AOL, for example. Google offers a free site that lets you check your rankings: http://www.googlerankings.com.

It's easy to see why a combination of paid search and organic listings is essential to propel your small business forward. It's also clear that it takes patience before conversions are fully realized. In fact, search engine conversions show up long after initial search queries. Consider this: A ComScore Networks study examining the impact of search engine usage on the purchase of consumer electronics and computer products showed that among consumers who chose to purchase online following a search, 85 percent of the sales occurred in a later (non-search) session.[7]

#13 PLACE ONLINE ADVERTISING

Paid search is only one component of online advertising—though it seems to get the most attention. If you're looking for a way to add a cost-effective component with an easily trackable ROI to your marketing program, the Web can be a powerhouse of affordable advertising. In fact, local ad spending was projected to reach nearly $4 billion nationwide in 2005.

For small businesses that market exclusively on the Web, strategically placed online ads will drive site traffic and build company or brand awareness while generating leads and sales. And for multi-channel marketers, complete integration of online and off-line advertising messages will ensure your customers have a consistently positive shopping experience. With the flexibility of the Web and superior reporting tools, you can run a variety of long-term promotions on different sites or run a single limited-time promotion across numerous sites. Then evaluate their performance—from click-through to conversion—to build an increasingly successful program.

Advertising creation, whether online or off-line, is rarely a do-it-yourself job. So you'll want to work with an advertising team that's experienced in executing online creative. Online ads must deliver a lot of punch using very little copy in a small space, much like outdoor billboards, and one of their chief functions is to successfully stimulate click-through.

Five Steps to Placing Your Own Campaign

The good news is, you can hire creative talent to develop your ads yet save considerable dollars by placing your campaign yourself by following these five steps:

I. Find the right sites. Haven't a clue where you might advertise? Start by performing searches on the keyword phrases your prospects might use to find your site. Note the sites that accept advertising and are not directly competitive with yours. This is a great way to get an overview of Web sites with well targeted, or at least highly relevant, content. You'll turn up a variety of Web portals, some of them entirely vertical and dedicated to a particular industry or interest, such as boating or organic farming, as well as others that provide general news and information.

For starters, you'll have a long list of sites on which you could potentially advertise. Next, it's time to begin narrowing your search to just the sites that can demonstrate your audience visits in sufficient numbers. If you're targeting your local market, consider the online edition of your daily paper. Local newspapers have the leading Web sites in 74 of the 81 metropolitan markets regularly surveyed, according to The Media Audit.[8]

Some sites are self-selecting simply based on the subject matter (Boating.com would be a good example), while other sites may be able to give you excellent data drawn from the lifestyle or demographic information visitors supplied when they registered. So contact the advertising sales representatives for the sites that you believe will best serve your needs and ask them for visitor statistics.

Relevant subject matter is one reason you'll see the makers of Sea Eagle inflatable boats and kayaks, Harrison-Hoge Industries, Inc., of Port Jefferson, New York, advertising on Web portal, Paddling .net. President Cecil Hoge, Jr., and his brother, Vice President John Hoge, run an extensive multichannel marketing campaign that includes off-line print advertising, cataloging, paid search, and other online advertising. These adept marketers jumped on the Internet in the 1990s, and saw online sales alone climb from $6,000 in 1996 to $3 million in 2004. The company's advertising sponsorship on Paddling.net gives them a link to one of their sites, SeaEagle.com, which John Hoge credits with helping his company achieve a higher organic ranking on Google. (You'll see more about these fascinating marketers and their family legacy of small business success in Chapter 10.)

2. Evaluate the advertising "environment." Not only is it important to learn all you can about each site's visitors, you need to gather additional information about how users interact with the sites. Look at the number of "unique visitors" as well as "total pages viewed," which will give you an idea of whether visitors look at one page or several in a session. On the Internet, just as in other forms of advertising, frequency matters, particularly when it comes to elevating awareness for a company or brand. Ads often start to be effective after several exposures, so ideally the sites you choose should give you an opportunity to build frequency with individual visitors. This can be achieved in two ways: either you'll reach the same visitors as they return to the site repeatedly over time, or make a strong impression with visitors who go to numerous pages on the site (where they can see your ads) in a single session.

3. Explore your advertising opportunities. As you evaluate a variety of Web sites, you'll see that some offer a better shot at reaching just the right prospects for your company. Often this is accomplished by providing advertising "channels," or groups of pages on a Web site, that contain content that meets the unique needs of a specific type of reader. For example, the Web site for the major daily newspaper *The Washington Post,* http://www.thewashingtonpost.com, offers online channels that are actually narrower than the print sections of the newspaper. There's one channel just called "Washtech," so if you were trying to reach companies selling to the federal government, you'd want your ads to appear there. Choosing to advertise in a highly targeted channel may cost a premium, but it effectively allows you to target just the readers who will be predisposed to your message. Most important, it ensures your advertising will appear in the right context. When you buy advertising in a channel or in a fixed position, you pay a set price per month that does not depend on the traffic.

Other sites allow you additional, highly sophisticated targeting options. As a small-business owner, you may be familiar with the *Business Journal* newspapers that are published in cities nationwide. You can place ads on their online Web portal, http://www.bizjournals.com, or in their e-mail newsletters and target your specific audience by market, industry, day of the week, and more. They also provide a do-it-yourself interface small-business advertisers can use to design and track their online ads.

Yet the most typical online advertising buy is called ROS, which stands for "run of site." And when you begin to look at advertising rates, you'll see ROS rates posted based on the cost-per-thousand (CPM) impressions. A good rule of thumb is to buy the number of impressions you need, starting with a conservative number (the sales reps can guide you here) and then adjust. By making an ROS buy, you give the site publisher the permission to place your ads on whichever pages have space available, so you may need to buy a fixed position on the main page plus ROS in order to reach visitors more than once.

One thing to bear in mind when making an ROS buy is that many publishers only allow select ad sizes to run on certain pages. In other words, while they may accept a skyscraper (120 × 600 pixels) on the main page, you may also need to design a square button ad (125 × 125 pixels) or a banner to run elsewhere.

4. Negotiate a package. Once you have reviewed the data and rates from the sites on which you plan to place advertising, you'll be ready to negotiate with the reps and make your buys. You may be surprised to learn that rate cards are not necessarily firm online, although newspaper sites are less negotiable than many others. Typically, the more you buy, the lower the CPM. Now is the time to explore deals that you can make through combo buys, such as by advertising in an e-newsletter (more about this later in this chapter) on the same publisher's Web site or in a related print publication (if it has one).

You may also run into different pricing models, including CPC (cost-per-click)—you only pay when someone clicks through—and CPA (cost-per-action). With CPA, you and the publisher determine what constitutes an "action" and then you pay according to a pre-negotiated agreement.

5. Track your results. One of online advertising's most superior attributes is its measurability. Successful marketers track and measure every aspect of their online advertising results. And the best way to do so is by using "ad serving" software if you have your own dedicated server or by having your ads "served" by a hosting company. Here's how it works: When your ads are served by a hosting company, each time a Web page containing one of your ads is displayed, a small bit of computer code instructs it to download from the independent server. And each ad download equals one "impression."

Fortunately, this is another vital service that has now become available to small businesses at a remarkably affordable cost—sometimes from as little as $10 per month, depending on the number of impressions served. Having your ads served is invaluable if you're running on multiple sites. You gain essential information, including the number of impressions delivered, the number of click-throughs, the time of day, and the day of the week activity occurs. With this in-depth information, you'll be able to fine-tune your ad program by eliminating nonperformers and increasing your activity on the Web sites that produce best. You'll also be able to gauge the effectiveness of individual offers and your ad creative.

#14 MARKET THROUGH THIRD-PARTY E-NEWSLETTERS

Want a form of advertising that carries an implied endorsement? Then you should consider placing ads in subscriber newsletters. This is currently the single best way to use e-mail as a customer acquisition tool. Here's why:

- Your ad appears in a less-cluttered environment with only one or two other advertisers.
- The deliverability is higher because your ad is in content that people have requested.
- Subscriber e-mails are less affected by spam filters.
- You can build advertising frequency with a loyal readership.
- Subscriber newsletters are excellent for time-sensitive offers, from trade show promotions to ads for seminars.

In fact, the bottom line is that advertising in subscriber newsletters can be more effective than ads placed on Web sites. And the cost can be attractive, too. While the CPM for ads placed in subscriber newsletters versus on Web sites may be higher because of their typically lower circulation (or number of impressions), the ad units themselves are usually less expensive. So if you're on a tight budget, you may be able to place ads in highly targeted and well-read subscriber newsletters for less overall than placing ads on the sites from which they originate. Also, the longer you advertise (or the larger your buy), the lower the CPM you may be able to acquire. For example, the *Business Journals* offer several e-newsletters priced at $65/M for the first four weeks of advertising, but the CPM drops to $60/M when you sign for an additional month, and keeps dropping until it reaches $45/M for 52 weeks.

Of course, the ideal program is an integrated one—surrounding the prospect from a variety of angles—such as by advertising on a publisher's site, in its newsletter, and possibly also combining that purchase with off-line advertising in a related publication. Conduct your search for the right online e-newsletters the same way you would investigate potential advertising opportunities on Web sites. Many major Web portals, newspaper and magazine publishers, and even cable TV networks offer subscriber e-newsletters, and it's merely a matter of finding the ones that best target your audience and in which you can afford to advertise with sufficient frequency.

#15 MAXIMIZE RETURNS FROM INCOME-GENERATING PROGRAMS

So far, throughout these chapters I've hammered home the notion of placing your ads where they'll be surrounded by relevant content. That's the concept behind the "contextual advertising" programs run by Google, Yahoo!, and others. Google, for example, offers a contextual ad program called AdSense that began basically as a bonus program for advertisers that ran pay-per-click listings. When you participate in the program, your display or text ads appear on Web pages that Google has deemed to carry appropriate content, including some of the largest and most highly trafficked sites on the Web. You choose from the available sites and bid on the ad space based on the cost-per-thousand impressions, rather than on a cost-per-click basis. So small-business owners, with very little expense, can reach prospects anywhere on the Web who are actively interested in content that relates to what they have to sell.

Veteran entrepreneur Mike Gariepy is president of plan3D, Inc. The company, which he started in October of 2001, is his latest brainchild. It offers a home design software product that works on a Web page and allows users to virtually build a complete home, add landscaping, furnish it, and see it in photorealistic 3-D—something some skeptics said would be impossible to do. Subscriptions to use the software are sold on a yearly basis. This is the third business Gariepy has owned, and he spent several years writing the program before its launch. It was a tough challenge, but Gariepy was well prepared. Prior to founding plan3D, he owned a successful software company, which he says became ArtToday in 1996 and sold clip art on CDs until it was purchased by Jupiter Media in July of 2003 for $18 million.

To build sales for his growing business, Gariepy has focused on a program of pay-per-click advertising using Yahoo! Search Marketing Solutions and Google AdWords and AdSense programs, employing as many as 400 to 500 keyword phrases such as "online interior design." In addition to the ads that appear in search engine results, his contextual ads run in relevant content on many publishers' Web pages—including on such megasites as iVillage.com, where other advertisers are paying thousands of dollars per ad. With about 8,000 clicks on his ads per day from his pay-per-click campaign, Gariepy says he receives a 2 percent conversion rate at a cost of 9 cents per click through to his Web site, plan3D.com—which he deems a good return on his investment.

Like Gariepy, you can participate in the contextual ad programs offered by major players, Google and Yahoo. Or you can choose to market your products and services through programs offered by other companies, including Kanoodle, that focus on "vertical" categories to build click-through. But did you know that you can use a contextual advertising program to generate income directly from your Web site at zero cost?

As a Web site publisher, you can have contextual ads appear on your Web pages and receive income every time your visitors click on them. For example, here's how Google's AdSense program works: When you sign up as a publisher and your site is approved, you receive 1 percent to 3 percent of the amount paid for clicks on Google ads on your Web site. The ads that appear are relevant because they're matched to your page content, and you can place them on your main page, or any page on your site that you choose, by copying and pasting a small block of HTML. Keyword filters, although not foolproof, keep out inappropriate and competitive ads, and you can customize the appearance of the ads so that they blend with the other content on your site. Publishers have access to a report that includes the total number of impressions, ad clicks, click-through rate, effective CPM, and total earnings. Best of all, at this writing, there's no cost to participate as a Web site publisher in this type of contextual advertising program and it takes a minimal investment of time to manage.

Another entirely free way to earn income from your Web site is by working with a major "affiliate" marketing company, such as Commission Junction, and placing links from advertisers on your site. There's little maintenance involved. The links are served and tracked by Commission Junction, which calculates the commission due, sends you payment, and provides a suite of online tools. Like the major contextual ad programs, there's no cost for site owners. Once you're accepted into the program, you can choose the affiliate offers you wish to publish, including those of well-known national advertisers, and begin earning income on leads and sales.

The program works well for Bob Jameson, owner of Aurora Pages Press in Kenai, Alaska, who is a proponent of Commission Junction. The publisher of numerous well-trafficked Web sites, including Campgrounds-Alaska.com and AlaskanOutdoorPages.com, Jameson says he affiliates with 54 advertisers, adding to and deleting from the list based on performance. The affiliates whose ads Jameson chooses to display are appropriate for the content of his sites. To give you an idea of how your company can benefit from links from national advertisers with high-quality sites and earn income as well, here's a look at some of Jameson's top affiliates, listed in order of returns from February of 2005:

1. GoodSamClub.com
2. SeaEagle.com
3. Maps.com
4. Interland.com
5. Overture.com
6. Yahoo.com
7. AlaskaAir.com
8. Trails.com
9. Overtons.com
10. CruiseDirect.com

11. BassPro.com
12. SportsmansGuide.com

Affiliate marketing programs offered by reputable and well-established service companies can take the effort and expense out of running an affiliate program while earning income for your business. But that isn't always the case for do-it-yourself programs. For many small-business owners, the investment of time and money, plus legal considerations, simply don't warrant the modest return on investment of affiliate programs created in-house.

Web site owners with in-house affiliate marketing programs receive a commission from advertisers (or affiliate partners) on a cost-per-action basis—the specific type of action that results in payment is negotiable. A significant amount of effort is involved in recruiting and managing your affiliates, from identifying prospects to sending e-mails and making telephone calls, and tracking software, or an outside service, is required to measure and reward results. Plus, once your visitors click through from your site to an affiliate's, it's difficult to police how those leads are cared for. You may be potentially liable, according to the Federal Trade Commission, if your affiliates become spammers and send e-mail that violates the law—not the best way to build a successful business.

#16 LAUNCH A BLOG

Blogging is a relatively new, yet growing Internet phenomenon, and by the spring of 2005, 11 million people, or 1 out of every 17 American citizens, had created a blog, according to a Pew Internet and American Life Project study.[9] Creating your own company blog (short for Web log) can be an excellent way to foster a feeling of one-to-one communication with customers and prospects who visit your Web site, raise your company visibility, provide product or service details and news, and build repeat visits to your site. Much depends on your target audience, as young adults are more likely to read blogs than are older adults, particularly seniors. A CNN/USA Today/Gallup Poll in March of 2005 showed that nearly 75 percent of all blog readers were age 49 or younger, with one-quarter in the 18 to 29 age group.[10]

There are blogs in virtually every vertical industry. Just check out a blog directory, such as http://www.blogpulse.com, which lets you search millions of blogs for postings related to specific topics. You can create your own blog using software such as Blosxom (blosxom .com) and Movable Type (movabletype.org), which are two of the most popular.

There's a certain nuance to creating a blog visitors want to read. Rather than an opportunity to overtly promote or sell, your company blog is a way to share news and opinions—perhaps even be a bit controversial. When you create your own blog, you can immediately post information, establish a dialogue, propose solutions and suggestions for product and service issues, and easily link to other related online sources.

Successful bloggers suggest that you post regularly, and when negative issues surface regarding your company or its products and services, it's important to quickly address them in your posts to build long-term trust. If what you say is interesting, helpful, or thought-provoking, you'll get people talking. Blogs become popular when published posts are referenced by other bloggers, syndicated via feed aggregators, and linked to by more well-known blogs. And once your blog is a hit, you can accept advertising—and create an entirely new revenue stream.

4

MAKE PR PROFITABLE

Have you read the story of the fledgling company that was struggling to be noticed until PR put it on the map? In this chapter you will. In fact, if you're looking for smart, low-cost ideas, the small-business owners included in this chapter will supply plenty. And you'll learn how the power of successful media coverage or even building buzz through word of mouth can put your company on the radar screens of important customers and prospects.

#17 ESTABLISH A
MEDIA RELATIONS PROGRAM

More than 20 years ago, when I was director of development of a marketing communications company, I had a boss who was fond of saying that public relations was just doing good and telling about it. Now, more than ever before, we live in a world of 24/7 news and information where there's an outlet for every type of story. Thanks to the "demassification" of America and proliferation of niche media, no matter what group you target, today there's a published forum in which to reach it.

Television media opportunities encompass programming from network, cable, and local news to national and local talk shows. In other words, there's everything from CNN, the *Oprah Winfrey Show,* and *Good Morning America* to big budget local programs such as *Good Day LA* or even shows on local public access. And let's not overlook all the how-to and lifestyle programming on the cable networks. Have a new stenciling kit that's perfect for home decor use? Perhaps you can get booked as a guest on do-it-yourself or home design shows. For small-business owners without the capital to place television campaigns, media relations programs targeting select producers can get you booked on just the right shows and transform a relatively invisible company or product into a desirable commodity.

Like TV, radio has always afforded excellent public relations opportunities through both talk and news programming. But it's print media that has lately been most transformed thanks to "media diversity." There's a print publication for every message and every market, whether they're trade publications, consumer magazines, or newspapers. And the Internet now provides a vast array of new public relations opportunities, from placing articles on Web sites, garnering product reviews and editorials, to creating buzz via blogs.

Clearly, if PR is doing good and telling about it, then media relations is about connecting with exactly the journalists, producers, or editors who can tell your story to the right audiences. A good media relations program can propel a small start-up business into a multimillion-dollar, national success. That was indeed the case for Fran's Chocolates, Ltd. This Seattle, Washington–based company was started in 1982 as a retail store by its president and founder, Fran Bigelow, who likened her confections to the fine chocolates available in Europe. Bigelow says the chocolates of choice on the grocery store shelves at that time were Hershey's and Baker's, so she began what she calls an "educational mission," training everyone who worked in her shop to talk to each customer who came through the door about her high-quality chocolate products.

Bigelow's store was in an out-of-the-way location, which meant she'd have to make it a primary destination by reaching out to customers who were willing to make the extra effort to visit. Because she lacked a major advertising budget, she decided to target the food editors of the two Seattle papers. Bigelow visited their offices, where she presented each with samples and a letter and invited them to her shop. As a result, both papers published stories about Fran's Chocolates and customers were soon standing in line to buy her chocolates.

Those articles spurred other members of the media, including the food editor for *Sunset Magazine,* to seek out Fran's Chocolates. And in 1986, Bigelow got another opportunity to win press coverage by participating in a tasting during a food writers' conference held in Seattle. What followed was coverage in numerous publications, including the *Chicago Tribune* and the *Baltimore Sun.* From this, Bigelow has created an ongoing media relations program, maintaining contact with journalists nationwide. Fortunately, Bigelow says her product is a natural fit for the media, who look forward to receiving her recipes for Valentine's Day, Mother's Day, and other holidays and events, such as graduation. She also introduces new products every year and continually researches new recipes and flavors.

Today, Fran's Chocolates are sold through its two shops, a catalog, and a Web site, plus they are distributed wholesale to food and gourmet stores. Yet with a staff of 35 and projected 2005 sales of more than $4 million, Bigelow says Fran's Chocolates still relies on media relations. In 1996, the *Book of Chocolate* named Fran's Chocolates "the best chocolatier in America," further enhancing Bigelow's national image as a chocolate expert. And in 2004, she published her own book, *Pure Chocolate,* with Random House. After more than 20 years of growth, it's safe to say that media relations transformed an unknown, out-of-the-way shop and its owner into a stunning success.

Not only can media relations get a new business off to a successful start, it can breathe life back into one that has all but closed its doors. When Tom Tagtmeyer and his two partners bought Modern Bin on April Fools' Day in 2004, the company, which had been around since 1947, had just three remaining employees and sales of $70,000 a month. Modern Bin is a material handling company that sells anything required to set up a warehouse, including shelving, workbenches, and lockers. The owner of this Savage, Minnesota, company was retiring and had given everyone notice. But the partners, who come from diverse business backgrounds, saw a venerable name with a solid brand and believed they could buy the company and turn it around.

In the summer of 2004, Tagtmeyer and his partners hired a small PR firm to target all local media. Their hook—local jobs saved and added in a down economy—had the effect of getting people in the community to "root for the home team," Tagtmeyer says. The coverage made the phone ring and produced enough sales to encourage Modern Bin's owners and their PR firm to come up with the idea for a back-to-school special that would attract even more media coverage.

The partners brought in 3,000 school lockers, some to be refurbished and some new, and invited the media to come and view their crew preparing lockers for schools all over Minnesota. Fox Channel 9 News sent a TV news crew and aired the Modern Bin story six times over the course of a day as the construction of the lockers progressed. The coverage made the new business partners into local heroes, depicting them as individuals coming in to save people's jobs. The TV coverage produced another benefit: It introduced Modern Bin to a new consumer market, allowing the company to sell lockers and shelving for children's rooms and garages. Plus, all the print and broadcast media coverage helped the company rebuild its credibility and recruit top staff.

In 2005, Modern Bin had projected sales of $5.5 million and a core staff of 23 that swelled to nearly 40 when the company was at its busiest. The resurrected business boasts a solid customer base, including 3M, Miller Brewing, and St. Jude Medical Center. And because of the firm's rapid growth, Tagtmeyer said it's beginning to get a whole new kind of media coverage—it seems the partners have become recognized experts on how to turn a business around.

Four Steps to Creating a Media Relations Program

Are you ready to devise your own media relations program? Just follow these four basic steps:

1. **Start with a clear goal.** Like any effective marketing program, a media relations campaign should be designed based on a strong company goal. What do you want to happen as a result of your program? Do you want to raise awareness of your business, position yourself or your company as expert, enhance your image to recruit quality personnel, launch a new product or service? It may take some months for your media relations program to take hold, so choose a long-term goal that's realistic and achievable.

2. **Define your story.** Consider your media relations goal and choose a story angle that will aim the spotlight where it's needed. Suppose you wanted to use media relations to launch a new product. You'd need a strong story angle, probably one that included how this new product would benefit its users in a whole new way. This story angle would be designed to appeal to the press and would be hammered home in all media communications until it was picked up with enough frequency. Then your story could evolve into showing customer interaction with your product and so on through the life of your media campaign. One small-business owner who recently introduced a line of organic cosmetics achieved media relations success by promoting the product "category" (cosmetics with organic ingredients) first. She touted the health reasons behind the use of organic cosmetics until she was seen as an expert and the story evolved to encompass her unique products.

3. Choose media to fit. Media outlets are inundated with press releases and other pitches—sometimes as many as thousands per day. The vast majority are discarded. Only the stories that will have particular appeal to a media outlet's readers, viewers, or listeners will even be considered. After all, the primary job of most media organizations is to increase subscriptions and newsstand sales, raise ratings, or sell more advertising.

Which media outlets will be most interested in the story you have to tell? Create your own media relations list by identifying your local, regional, or national media targets. For help, you can turn to directories, such as Bacon's MediaSource (bacons.com) and the free searchable database at Gebbie Press (gebbieinc.com).

4. Build relationships. Before you contact any of the media outlets, it's a smart idea to become familiar with their content so that you can tailor your story accordingly. And because media relations success rests on one-on-one interaction, it's vital to select key media; become familiar with their needs; provide materials to specific editors, producers, or journalists; and then follow up by phone or e-mail.

Media contact can be initiated using one of three basic formats: a press release, a media alert, or a pitch letter. A press release is generally designed to carry new or noteworthy information, while a media alert announces an event, such as a radio tour or an appearance by an author or celebrity. Not surprisingly, a pitch letter is sent to a journalist to describe (or pitch) a story idea.

You'll quickly discover that virtually all members of the media are continually pressed for time. Consequently, much of what they use comes from press releases that announce new studies or statistics, video news releases, radio tours, or photographs that have been supplied by businesses or their public relations firms. That means winning coverage often depends on going beyond a basic press release. You can provide a page of "tips" for journalists to quote from or use as a springboard for interviews with you. You can position yourself as expert in your field by scheduling a radio tour on a newsworthy topic, supplying professional-quality product photographs that can be easily inserted into magazines or newspapers, or win high-tech reviews by e-mailing links to an online demo.

#18 ADD ONLINE PR

Why build a media relations program focused exclusively on off-line media, when you can easily add an online component as well? Look for Web sites that are frequented by your target audience and that could carry your story in the appropriate context. Create an online media list and contact the editors via e-mail. Just like off-line media, what you pitch will depend on your public relations goal. You may target sites that carry product reviews and offer product samples or online demos, or perhaps you would like to position yourself as an expert in your field and provide articles that will carry your byline.

Online columnists and freelance journalists often supply their e-mail addresses in their bylines. So if you have a story you think a journalist will find particularly interesting, you can contact her by e-mail with a brief overview and an attached press release. Just be sure you've done your homework and familiarized yourself with the type of story the writer can use. Once you get a response, you can maintain an ongoing relationship by e-mail or set up a time to talk by phone.

You can even get PR coverage from blogs. Some PR firms now specialize in reaching opinion sites and blogs, but you can also place your own PR by following a few important guidelines. Locate sites with relevant content using blog search engines, such as http://www.blogsearchengine.com/directory.html. Because a mention in one key blog can mushroom into links to others on similar topics, start your media relations program by contacting the most popular and well-targeted blogs. Just as with off-line media, you should familiarize yourself with each blog before making contact. Then, instead of sending a canned press release or pitch letter, send an e-mail that includes a link to a published story or item that the blogger might consider featuring. Bloggers can be a somewhat idiosyncratic group, so for media relations success, be sure to take their individual preferences and published "stances" into consideration.

In addition to media relations, online events, such as Webinars and chats, are excellent PR tools. Not only do they draw prospects and customers, the publicity surrounding them can make targeted online editors and other journalists take notice. For example, I recently gave a Webinar sponsored by a technology client and an online teleclass hosted by a major financial service provider. The teleclass was similar to a "typed" chat, but I spoke into my phone and attendees could hear me live through their computer speakers and submit questions by e-mail to a moderator. About 1,600 people registered for the Webinar and 400 signed up for the teleclass. For the Webinar, I first created a major trend report that contained in-depth information that both the press and the attendees would find valuable. A copy of the complete report was promised to all attendees as well as the media. Prior to the Webinar and teleclass, advance publicity included press releases focusing on the vital nature of the content, then select media were issued invitations to attend.

Sometimes, "blasting" a release or media alert is called for. Instead of tailoring a story to a short list of key journalists, a blast is sent to thousands of publications and/or newsrooms through distribution services. Although not a substitute for effective media relations, blasting a release can get big, general news out to a vast number of potential outlets virtually instantly, particularly when using an online service such as PRNewswire.com, which will distribute your release via satellite directly into the computer networks at daily newspapers, news services, magazines, and television and radio stations. The cost of distributing your news release is determined by the geographic area you select and the length of your release. And PRNewswire's pricing, for example, starts at under $200 for city/metro or statewide distribution.

#19 CREATE A PRESS KIT

Once you've sent your initial materials and initiated follow-up or responded to inquiries by telephone or e-mail, you'll need a press kit to substantiate and embellish your story and provide journalists background information. But there's no need to hire a printer. This is one of those low-cost, high-impact tools that can be created quickly in-house, especially if you have an ink-jet color printer on hand. With ink-jet printers, which are quite inexpensive, you can create many full-color marketing materials in-house on a variety of paper stocks.

Basic Components of a Press Kit

Here are the components of a typical press kit:

1. **Carrier folder.** Some small-business owners think they need to have special folders to carry their press materials. This is an unnecessary expense. You can customize off-the-shelf folders that will work perfectly well for the media. The key is to start with a bright white, glossy, heavyweight, two-pocket folder that's die cut to hold a business card. You can buy this at most quality office-supply stores. To customize your folder, design and print out your cover art on glossy photo paper and apply double-stick tape on the back to adhere it to the front cover of your folder. The cover art you design can include a photo and text with your product or company name, or simply a color logo treatment, and the size can range from 8½ × 11-inch cover art to just a few inches square—it's up to you. Glossy paper works best because it blends in with the glossy white of the folder.

2. **Cover letter.** Because your press kit is a follow-up to a phone conversation, your letter should address the journalist by name, thank him or her for taking the time to speak with you, and immediately restate the news hook or pitch. Provide any substan-

tiating information or statistics in your cover letter, then close with a call to action stating that you will follow up soon by telephone.

3. Contents of the kit. In addition to your letter, include a copy of the original press release or media alert if you used one to initiate contact. The rest of the materials should be product, service, or company information, preferably in color and professionally produced. Include photographs where appropriate. Because the media are always more interested in companies that have received previous coverage from other sources, it's essential to include important press clips. Just don't overload the package. A major complaint from journalists is that they get pounds and pounds of materials they end up discarding because it's unnecessary or unrelated to the stories they're covering. So be sure to include only relevant materials and information. Of course, it's always a good idea to include a sample of what you're publicizing, if appropriate—this can be anything from a video, book, demo, or trial version of a product, or the product itself. But this should never be so large as to be misconstrued as an expensive "gift."

Ship your kits out quickly after a positive discussion with a journalist to ensure your story stays top-of-mind. Often, you'll need to send your kits by overnight delivery because of media deadlines. As you can see, creating and sending an effective press kit can get somewhat pricey—even when the artwork for the kit itself is assembled in-house—if you fail to use your kits judiciously. So reserve them exclusively for journalists or producers who've expressed an interest in receiving further information from you.

#20 ORGANIZE YOUR OWN PR RADIO TOUR

Have you ever been a guest on a radio call-in show or had an on-air interview? If you're a small-business owner who wants to build a reputation as an expert in a particular field, a public relations radio tour can make it happen. Radio tours are a great way to spread the word about a service business or educate audiences about the nuances of a new type of product. While, like all PR, on-air interviews are never an opportunity to directly sell, they position you as an expert in a field or product category, and discussions of your company's services or products often follow.

You can find an audience for just about any kind of topic. You've probably heard interviews with individuals in countless professions—all "experts" in the subject matter. On the radio, you might hear an environmental engineer talking about healthy homes, an accountant addressing ways to lower your taxes, a chiropractor being interviewed about perfect posture, or perhaps a fashion stylist giving tips on creating the best outfit for a first date.

It's also easy to target either business or consumer audiences with radio, simply by selecting the type of programming. There are all-business shows and also general consumer news and talk programming that reach consumers and some business audiences as well.

Radio tours are a mainstay tactic used by public relations agencies for placing on-air stories and garnering millions of gross impressions. When the interview is conducted by an agency, the expert being interviewed is generally made available by phone for a block of several hours on a given day. Then the "bookers" schedule interviews about every ten minutes during that time frame. The PR firm also has an outside producer coordinating the interviews who speaks with the stations while the expert is on the air. This producer lets the expert know which stations and interviewers are coming up next, and generally keeps things on track.

That's the *big-budget* way of conducting a radio tour. As an on-air spokesperson for numerous leading companies, including Visa, eBay, Hewlett-Packard, and Sprint, I've had the benefit of working on successful, professionally produced tours. But as an author and small-business expert promoting my books, I've also created my own radio tours with no expense except the time invested.

Create Your Own Radio Tour

Now I'll walk you step-by-step through the process of creating a radio tour to promote yourself and your company.

Step 1. Find a great hook. The hook is what will draw the media's attention to what you have to say. New numbers, facts, or statistics often make good hooks because they're considered newsworthy. Suppose your company specialized in fingerprinting and photographing small children to help ensure their safe return if lost or missing. Your news hook might be the statistical number of kindergarten and primary school-age children who become missing each year. Then you could provide expert insight into the types of safety precautions parents and teachers can take. For maximum bookings, you could schedule your tour to coincide with media interest in back-to-school stories.

Step 2. Create a media alert. This is a one-page announcement of your availability for interviews. It resembles a press release in a couple of ways: It has contact information at the top, a headline (based on your hook) that draws the recipient into your story, and one or two paragraphs that explain the issue/topic and why it's important. But next, unlike a press release, a media alert introduces the expert (you) with a brief overview of your credentials and announces your availability for interviews. While professionally booked media tours are generally scheduled for a several-hour time period on a specific date, your tour need not be compressed in that way. This can actually work to your benefit, because stations often have difficulty scheduling within a narrow time frame.

Step 3. Compile your list of targeted producers. This is going to take a bit of detective work. For a local tour, you can simply contact the radio stations to obtain the names of the producers of appropriate shows. Ideally, for a national tour you want to be interviewed by the major radio networks and independent stations in the top 25 markets. This would give you the maximum number of gross impressions, based on the number of listeners each station averages in the quarter hour during which your interview airs. (When I was a spokesperson for Sprint, one highly successful radio tour yielded 18 million gross impressions.) While it's rare for the average tour to entirely achieve this goal, this gives you an idea of what to shoot for.

You can use print publications (check the reference section of a major business library) and online resources, such as http://radiolocator.com, to compile your list. Radiolocator.com, for example, has a searchable database of radio stations with links to their Web sites. You can search for stations by format, such as news/talk; advanced searching lets you organize your results by state, so you can pick out the stations in the top markets. Check each station's Web site to find appropriate programming, then contact it by phone to get the name(s) of the producer(s).

Step 4. Write your PR platform. Advance preparation is the key to successful interviews. The job of most interviewers is to elicit information that will be of special interest to their listeners. So your top priority is to provide the relevant content they need while at the same time weaving in your own principal public relations themes. What are the primary messages you want to convey about your company or its products and services? Just review your own advertising, brochures, and Web content and choose three of the primary themes or copy points. Next, write a one-paragraph, three-point platform that conveys your central themes in a way that also meets the needs of listeners.

Your platform becomes your guide to keep you from straying off your message. It's an essential tool for a radio tour, since you may need to express the same central ideas in 20 or more interviews. Also, prepare answers to typical questions in advance of your interviews, and have someone test you with likely questions until your delivery is smooth, confident, and conversational.

Step 5. Send your alert. Once you're entirely prepared to handle interviews, you can send your alert to the media. Generally, alerts are sent via fax or e-mail, depending on the preferences of the producers. If you have an extensive list of recipients, it's a good idea to send them out in small batches. Send only as many at once as you can comfortably follow up by telephone within 24 hours.

Just as with any PR placement, this phone follow-up is vital. Consider your media alert a knock at the door. Once the door is open, you have an opportunity to pitch your story and close for an interview. It's also a chance to establish a relationship that may lead to multiple interviews over time.

Step 6. Give a great interview. A terrific interview meets the needs of the interviewer and the audience plus conveys your central messages. No matter what you're asked, you should always be able to *bridge back* to one of the three central points in your platform. *Bridging* is the term used to describe giving an answer that links one subject to another—preferably the topic you want to address. Suppose you own a landscape design firm in Arizona that specializes in using native plants that require little supplemental water, and a radio interviewer asks you a question about how to maintain a healthy lawn in a desert environment. You'd reply by providing a brief fact about the water requirements of the average lawn, and then bridge directly to one of the points in your platform such as the household savings and community-wide advantages of conserving water through use of native plant materials instead of lawns.

Although some radio interviews will be aired live, you should expect many to be taped and then edited for later broadcast. So keep your answers short and concise to ensure your key messages survive the editing process without being garbled or lost. And here's a technical tip: Radio producers prefer you use a landline and a corded (not cordless) phone. A headset with a noise-canceling microphone is also a plus, but some producers may prefer the sound quality if you speak directly into a standard handset.

#21 DESIGN AN EVENT

Many small-business owners "dabble" in special events, but few get the bang for the buck they really need. The problem is, participating in many events—from community fairs to charity balls—can simply spread you and your message too thin. The solution is to design your own event that throws the spotlight on your company alone.

Terrific examples of publicity garnered through special events are everywhere you look. Here are two to get you thinking:

> A small photography studio locates in a run-down inner-city building and participates in the rehabilitation of the area. Its owners throw a party to celebrate the completion of the project, at the same time treating visitors to a gallery display of their new work. The corresponding PR effort yields: coverage in the local business press, the national trade press, and a national cable television show, and positive reviews of the gallery display in the arts-and-leisure section of the local newspaper.

> When a custom home building and remodeling company opens a kitchen and bath showroom in its hometown, it marks the first time the local residents can shop for upscale appliances and fixtures without driving 90 minutes to a major city. The party, whose theme is based on the historic and quaint nature of the local area, draws interior designers, homeowners, and the press. And it produces sufficient coverage and public attention to make the entire targeted segments of the local community aware of the new showroom.

Public Relations Guidelines

Creating a terrific event doesn't have to cost a lot. The party budget itself can be modest so long as participants enjoy themselves. Just be sure to follow some public relations guidelines:

Pick a strong theme. Your event should have a purpose or goal and a theme to match. What will be your primary hook?

Do prepublicity and postpublicity. Like in the example of the event hosted in the photography studio, yours may appeal to several types of media with very different story angles. Send press releases and invitations in advance of your event, and win publicity following the event as well by sending photographs and press releases or pitching follow-up stories to additional media. If there is a "larger" story, work with individual journalists on in-depth pieces.

Employ a media liaison. Prior to the event, prepare a platform or even a simple message that you want members of the media to take away. Then, during the event have your media liaison communicate directly with all the members of the press. And be sure to supply press kits. If your event is large enough, you may need to set aside a separate staging area strictly for members of the press and schedule a time for photos.

A year after Connie Chantilis's company opened its first storefront location, it experienced a severe identity problem. After six years in business, Dallas-based Two Sisters Catering needed to convince its varied target audience that it could do more than cater small events and run a box-lunch business. So Chantilis's solution was to throw a large party showcasing the kind of elegant menu and decor her company could provide. Hundreds of guests turned out and tremendous press coverage followed, prompting Chantilis to make the party an annual event, drawing as many as 500 to 700 people. Each year, they rolled out something new, whether it was six different soup stations or a dazzling dessert selection.

Unlike during the company's early years, today Chantilis's annual parties are now underwritten by local umbrella charities. In this way, Two Sisters Catering creates a function for the charities and wins even greater goodwill from their members and the community. From a publicity standpoint, the charity affiliation is smart, too. Prior to each event, the charity sends out a release and handles prepromotion, and following the event, the company receives coverage in the society page of the newspaper.

Two Sisters Catering has two people on staff designated as press liaisons, and sends out frequent releases as well as a monthly e-mail newsletter that goes to the press and the customer base. The e-newsletter contains recipes, news of charity events and cooking classes, plus entertaining tips. With projected company sales of $2.75 million in 2005, Chantilis says Two Sisters receives two or three calls every month from the media. The *Dallas Business Journal* has recognized Two Sisters Catering as the "Best Caterer in Dallas." And it's safe to say that Chantilis's PR efforts have obliterated any past identity crisis.

Not ready to throw a party? Organize a race, host a golf tournament, or create your own basketball team. Sound far-fetched? Just ask Constantine Pergantis, president of Nite Lites, an exterior lighting contracting company based in the Washington, D.C., suburb of Bethesda, Maryland. When he founded his company in 1988, Pergantis was about 25 years old and needed a way to make his company look bigger and more credible. He also had very little money to put into marketing. A self-described "frustrated basketball player," he decided to put together a team and sponsor it. He gave the three-on-three basketball team his company name, the Nite Lites, and they've been playing steadily all across the country for the past 17 years, each year getting bigger and better players. The team plays on weekends, with four to six events a year.

Now before you get the idea that Pergantis's company has the deep pockets of a major sporting sponsor, you should know that Nite Lites has sales of about half a million dollars annually with four full-time and three part-time employees. Many of its customers are and were pro basketball players. Pergantis credits his company's success and longevity to his intensive PR campaign and the media "hook" it provides. He says, "I figured the more I could get the name in the paper, the more they'd remember me."

Pergantis's strategy is to contact local media in the cities the team travels to, as well as in his hometown of metropolitan D.C., asserting that the "Nite Lites are coming and we're going to win." In some cases, stories run in the media prior to the team's arrival, and at other times postpublicity hits following the tournaments. Pergantis sends e-mail to radio, TV, and newspaper journalists in the cities where his team plays. Of course, he says it helps to have good players and a few that were known in the college and semi-pro ranks, plus high-profile athletes as customers. As a result of this coverage, Pergantis has installed commercial and residential lighting projects as far north as Hartford, Cleveland, New York City, and Philadelphia, as far south as Richmond, Atlanta, Orlando, and Miami, and even out west in Dallas.

When his team receives coverage in an important paper, Pergantis also sends e-mails with the news to his customer and prospect lists. This helps to build referrals and up-sell past customers. So Pergantis wins new customers and up-sells his existing customer base—and he gets to have fun doing it.

#22 BUILD GRASSROOTS BUZZ

When a Mexican restaurant in San Francisco offered free lunch for life to anyone who got a tattoo of its flamboyant "Jimmy the Corn Man" logo, 39 people actually accepted the challenge. This was so outrageous, the restaurant received coverage in *USA Today* and other major media—all for just the cost of burritos. On a bit larger scale, in March of 2005, the NBC Agency staged a stunting event for its TV series, *The Office*, a humorous look at the nine-to-five world. Men dressed in business suits wearing sandwich boards that stated "My Boss Sucks " walked up and down in high pedestrian traffic areas in the business sectors of cities including San Francisco, Chicago, New York, Seattle, Philadelphia, and Boston. Get the idea?

It doesn't have to cost a lot to make a big splash that will build buzz for your small business. When coming up with a grassroots approach to build word of mouth, the key is to reach your target audience in a creative way, but keep the activities you undertake consistent with the image you wish to convey.

Constantine Pergantis is a wizard at fueling buzz. When he received a request from the local high school, which many of his customers' children attend, to put up several banners in the gymnasium for a group of very special events, he took that request and ran with it. Instead of putting up a few banners, Pergantis and his Nite Lites crew donated four days of work to put up 50 championship banners—from 1968 to the present day—in the school gym. Best of all, he created a fun story to pitch to the press, saying he went to a "rival" school and they would take his diploma away. He also "dropped" the name of a nationally recognized politician who would be attending the events.

Pergantis sent e-mails to three local newspapers and within two weeks they wrote articles about the banners and who put them up. There was even a photo of Nite Lites employees hanging the banners. Most important, when the school sent an e-mail to parents that included a special thank-you to Pergantis, he received "20 to 30 e-mails" from existing customers and prospects. And he immediately got two lighting jobs.

#23 GET "STAR POWER"
WITH A CELEBRITY SPOKESPERSON

What do John Travolta, Lauren Bacall, and Jessica and Ashlee Simpson have in common with Cal Ripken and many of the world's top athletes? They've all been endorsers or spokespersons for products or causes. Of course, stars may command endorsement fees in the millions, but other spokespeople, such as authors and industry experts, are available for considerably less.

To stand out at your next trade or consumer show, why not use a celebrity or expert to draw traffic to your booth? Hiring an outside endorser makes the most of what I call the "made you look" factor. For fees ranging from just around $2,000 to approximately $5,000 for an event, you can draw attention to your message and confer credibility by hiring a spokesperson. There's a never-ending array of top professionals from which to choose. Base your choice of spokesperson on your message and target audience. You can call on academics, retired athletes (though perhaps not superstars), authors (particularly those promoting new books), medical and other experts, actors or local celebrities for your special events and PR tours.

You can also use a celebrity spokesperson to draw customers to retail promotions. If you're a brick-and-mortar retailer, just promote the event using space in your regular advertising. Plus, send releases and invitations to the press along with special invitations to your customer base. Not only will the celebrity draw media attention, you're bound to get excellent customer attendance. Anything from in-store celebrity-driven workshops and demos to fashion shows can draw high traffic and build positive buzz. To find a celebrity spokesperson, visit Hollywood-madison.com, or for a technical expert, author, or academic, try searching a site that's designed for journalists, Profnet.com.

C h a p t e r

5

THINK OUTSIDE
THE BOX

Every December 31, millions of Americans ring in the new year in front of their television sets watching the ball drop in Times Square. And beyond the throngs of celebrants, what viewers see are the glimmering lights of the enormous billboards that tower above Broadway. The 11 ad spaces on One and Two Times Square are among the country's most effective and expensive ads, costing up to $350,000 a month, according to AdAge.com, and that doesn't include the cost to create and support these high-definition LED sign displays.

Do the advertisers get their money's worth? Forty million people visit Times Square each year and millions more are exposed to the billboards through other media. Two major TV networks broadcast in Times Square, ABC and MTV, and the locale is featured in numerous television shows, movies, magazines, and books. So people from all over the world are exposed to these enormously high-profile billboards. Not surprisingly, the majority of advertisers in Times Square, including Coca-Cola, Planters Nuts, and Target stores, have long-term, multiyear deals.

Outdoor advertising is hot, and billboards represent merely one form of this highly popular medium, which is collectively referred to as "out-of-home." It's an advertising medium that's at once very old—dating back to when town shopkeepers first put up pictorial signs—and cutting-edge, with exciting, new technology and venues. Out-of-home advertising revenues nearly doubled in the ten years from 1994 through 2004, when the industry generated $5.8 billion. What did advertisers purchase in 2004? According to the Outdoor Advertising Association of America, Inc., 62 percent was spent on billboards, 19 percent on transit, 14 percent on "street furniture," and 5 percent on what's being termed *alternative outdoor* (lots more about this later).

Times Square billboards may be the Mount Everest of out-of-home advertising, but the vast majority of other venues offer more down-to-earth pricing. In fact, out-of-home advertising—from billboards to ads on double-decker buses and posters in college dorms—is an effective and affordable way to market your small business.

#24 EXPLORE OUT-OF-HOME MARKETING

As you can imagine, each of the out-of-home "categories" contains many options. The billboards are easy to understand, but what about "street furniture"? This category includes bicycle rack displays, bus bench advertising, bus shelter panels, convenience and other in-store displays, kiosks, newsstand and news rack displays, and parking structure and shopping mall displays. Then, of course, there's transit advertising. Everyone's familiar with the signs both inside and outside buses, but don't forget subway and rail signage, airport displays, and the small, lighted signs atop taxis. In addition to these typical out-of-home advertising opportunities, there's currently a huge upsurge in other "place-based" advertising—everything from posters above diaper-changing stations to ads on the sides of the hospitality carts that cruise private golf courses.

Tips for Choosing Out-of-Home Opportunities

How can you choose the best out-of-home opportunities for your business? Consider these three criteria:

1. **Location.** If you're evaluating stationary media, such as a billboard or bus shelter, it must be located where you'll reach a high percentage of your prospects. Buying a billboard or subway poster on a monthly basis, for instance, can allow your target audience to see your message every day. So you'll reach a concentration of customers with considerable frequency. Investigate the visibility of each location you choose and the amount of traffic that will be exposed to your message. Bus shelters, for example, give you the advantage of having a six-foot poster at street level that can be seen by drivers as well as pedestrians waiting for the bus. Posters on bus exteriors are sold by the route based on the "showing," which is an estimate of the percentage of the population you're going to reach. You can choose to advertise on bus sides if you're targeting sidewalk traffic, or on bus backs to reach drivers.

Street furniture, even trash receptacles, can work if they put your message in front of the right prospects. Who would want to put their ad on a trash receptacle you ask? Actually, the receptacles are placed streetside in good locations and, although smaller, are similar in appearance to bus shelters. In Key West, Florida, for example, tourists often fall in love with the island and want to stay—or at least buy vacation homes there—and they are prime prospects for real estate agents. One of the best ways to reach these vacationers, who are in town for only a short while, is through advertising on street furniture. During the height of the tourist season, the trash receptacles along the major road leading into Old Town Key West all feature ads from real estate agents and brokers.

2. **The complexity of your message.** Not every advertising message is suited to outdoor media, although other types of out-of-home media may meet your needs. With billboards and most types of

outdoor signage, you must get your message across using a single strong visual image and just a few words. It's a form of visual storytelling. There's no opportunity to explain an offer or educate your audience in the few short seconds they'll be exposed to your message. The Outdoor Advertising Association of America recommends using fewer than seven words and three visual elements.

The best outdoor ads communicate a single benefit, often humorously, by combining a strong image and a headline. One billboard for Target stores included extensions (specially constructed elements that extend beyond the borders of the sign) and a fun headline to gain attention and featured the Looney Tunes characters Tweety and Sylvester. From a specially constructed extension, Sylvester the cat was peering down over the top of the billboard, shooting a hungry look at a blue Tweety Bird T-shirt on a giant hanger (another extension). The headline, which was a play on words, read "Tasty New School Clothes." The Target logo and name ran below the headline. Simple as that.

3. Price. Out-of-home advertising is one of the few marketing tactics that will match a local sales territory. You can put your message exactly where it will reach your prospects, tailoring your buy to eliminate waste. You can buy just a single outdoor billboard or 20 to reach commuters in Atlanta, and you can reach tourists in Key West with taxi-top ads or by advertising on the backs of the pedicabs that transport passengers up and down famous Duval Street in front of the bars and restaurants. This ability to pinpoint your prospects by using different types of advertising media in highly specific locations can make out-of-home advertising extremely cost-effective. You can choose the out-of-home advertising option that fits your type of business and budget. For some small-business owners, airport and shopping mall dioramas, which come with higher price points, are an exact fit for reaching the right audience in the right place at the right time, while outdoor billboards are often priced affordably enough for many types of small businesses with tighter budgets.

When small-business owner Shmuel Gordon and his partners in AHS Ventures LLC decided to launch HoustonConnect.com, an online site for singles in the city of Houston, they needed a high-impact advertising medium that would quickly spread the word to area singles and give their new company the credibility necessary to persuade local businesses to become advertisers and partners. Following the dot.com bust, Gordon says there was a pervasive misconception that "it didn't take much to have an Internet company." The partners wanted to send a message that they were professional and had an up-and-coming business. Plus, Gordon says, "We had to go to the masses."

Gordon is no stranger to starting and growing a business. Though just 30 years old, he is already a seasoned entrepreneur. One of his prior businesses, Progressive Systems (now called Lensec), became the number one provider of digital cameras for school districts in the country, and Gordon remains on its advisory board.

Almost immediately after launching HoustonConnect.com in July of 2003, Gordon established what was to become a highly effective outdoor ad campaign. In just a few short months, HoustonConnect .com became the number one singles site in Houston. In 2005, the site had projected sales of $1 million and by midyear already had 25,000 members. HoustonConnect.com offers a combination of free and paid memberships, with paid members gaining access to additional features. The ultimate goal for Gordon and his partners is to have local dating sites for singles in many cities, and plans are in the works for Dallas, Phoenix, Las Vegas, Atlanta, Denver, Philadelphia, Los Angeles, and other cities.

On a conservative budget, HoustonConnect.com relies on just two or three billboards a month, for about $3,000, and Gordon can directly trace their effectiveness. Every member who joins HoustonConnect.com must complete a required field letting the company know where he or she learned about the site, and billboards account for exactly 13.18 percent of memberships. According to Gordon, memberships in the local areas where the company has billboards are higher than in any others. He also credits the campaign with putting his company on the "business map," and says he rarely walks into a meeting where someone has not seen it. When his company approached Chipotle for a joint marketing campaign, they'd already seen the HoustonConnect.com billboards.

The outdoor campaign works synergistically with HoustonConnect .com's ongoing radio promotions. Rather than just run spots in rotation, Gordon and his partners comarket singles parties with Houston-area radio stations. (You'll learn a lot more about Gordon's radio campaign in Chapter 11.) Working together, the radio promotions and the high visibility of the billboards successfully build awareness and memberships.

In the course of the outdoor campaign, Gordon has learned what works and what doesn't when it comes to the creative on his billboards. What works: a big red heart over a white background that extends above the top of the billboard with the word "Single?" below it as the only headline. The URL, http://www.HousonConnect.com, runs quite prominently across the entire bottom of the billboard.

Want to know what hasn't worked? The headline "Chemistry Is Not Scientific" failed to pull a strong response because, Gordon says, "A lot of people drove by and didn't know what it meant." (Remember, there's no room to explain a concept on a billboard. Your message has to be instantly clear.) To create the art, Gordon simply e-mails his creative idea to Viacom Outdoor and the company prints it and custom builds the extension as part of his annual contract.

Viacom Outdoor, one of the three top players in the out-of-home industry, competes with Lamar Outdoor and Clear Channel Outdoor. Perhaps as many as half their collective advertisers are small businesses, including home developers, restaurants and entertainment venues, local auto dealers, and retailers such as appliance stores, bridal shops, furniture stores, insurance agencies, home repair and lawn and garden products and services. In fact, two of the most popular out-of-home advertising categories for small businesses are products and entertainment. A major plus for small businesses that are not working with agencies or are entering into

the out-of-home arena for the first time is that these outdoor companies will develop the creative concepts at no additional charge,
and build production costs for custom extensions and printing
into the monthly rate.

#25 CHOOSE THE NEWEST TECHNOLOGY

Right now, key billboards in many cities are being converted
to LED units. Lamar, for example, calls these "SMART Boards,"
and although advertising on them may be priced a bit higher, overall campaign costs are lower thanks to the elimination of printing
charges. What makes LED billboards revolutionary is that the
messages can be changed easily and frequently, even based on the
time of day. You can get results from one billboard in as little as
one month. And that's what the owners of Willow, a new restaurant
in Pittsburgh, were counting on when they chose to make a SMART
Board placement in the northbound lane of Interstate 279.

Part of their grand-opening announcement, this one-month
placement was chosen specifically to let potential north suburban
customers know about the new restaurant. Thanks to the flexibility of the SMART Board technology, Willow's owners were able
to change between three board images—even placing Willow's
happy-hour ads at specific times of the day.

Willow is the second of two restaurants featuring contempo-
rary American cuisine owned by Michael Rudman, Rick Stern,
and Greg Ackerman, who also own and operate Luma in downtown
Pittsburgh. They brought in Sheri Ward as director of sales and
marketing to help launch Willow, which opened July 30, 2004.
Ward created a successful campaign by combining a variety of
low-cost or free tactics, including outdoor. In mid-August through
September, once everything was running smoothly in the restaurant, Ward engineered a grand-opening party that was also a
fund-raiser for a nonprofit organization, and invited 1,500
guests, including local business and government leaders as well as

the press. She placed local newspaper and magazine advertising, including ads in *Pittsburgh* and *Whirl* magazines. To obtain free radio coverage, she brought food to the hosts of morning radio shows (who were already familiar with Luma and its chef). With this smart tactic, Ward successfully secured mentions on four radio stations.

Located just about ten minutes away from Willow on a busy interstate, the SMART Board was chosen because of its location and visibility. According to Ward, "It's all digital so the quality and visibility are excellent," and the images stood out particularly well at night. Willow simply supplied the photos and headlines and Lamar took care of the creative.

For one month, three interchanging boards appeared. On one, the headline "Everyone is talking about Willow" accompanied a photo of the dining area and the restaurant name and location. A second board featured the headline "Your table is ready" with a photo of a lovely, although empty, table along with the name of the restaurant and a phone number for reservations. The third, a happy-hour board, ran on Thursdays and Fridays at specific hours. It showed two people drinking wine and read simply "Happy Hour 5–7," along with the name of the restaurant and its location. Because Lamar had space available, the restaurant negotiated a special rate of $2,000 for the one-month placement, says Ward.

Ward and Willow's owners credit the successful launch in part to the effectiveness of the outdoor advertising. Ward says the SMART Board provided enough daily impressions to give Willow the reach it needed. Best of all—like Willow's now-popular crab cakes—it earned positive feedback from guests.

#26 BE INVENTIVE WITH PLACE-BASED MEDIA

When was the last time you left home and were in a truly advertising-free environment? Think about it. Now advertising messages go anywhere and everywhere people do. Go to almost any U.S. beach and you'll be greeted with a plane towing an ad banner. You may even be exposed to "beach sand impressions," which are ad messages imprinted into the sand and regenerated overnight. How about a ball game? Every conceivable stadium surface is covered with advertising, from signage to food snack packs, and some stadiums even have video screens built directly into the seat backs. Feel like going for a bike ride surrounded by nature? You may find your local biking trails are named after businesses, thanks to the new availability of naming rights for everything from nature trails to neighborhood swimming pools.

The industry calls this alternative out-of-home or placed-based media. And it's a bonanza for small businesses because there's literally something for everyone. While there are virtually limitless places to put your ads, here are just a few ideas to get you thinking:

- **Shopping cart returns**—advertising on the roof of shopping cart return stations located in supermarket parking lots.
- **Valet parking tickets**—messages are imprinted on all the segments.
- **Public telephones**—ads are placed on phone kiosks located near streetball courts and school yards, playgrounds, and urban parks to reach younger males when they're on the courts. (Of the 800,000 locations available, 1,500 are less than a block from a streetball court.)
- **Dry-cleaning bags and hangers**—ads are printed on garment bags, hangers, and paper covers.
- **Commercial restrooms**—posters located in public restrooms, such as in bars and restaurants, on stall doors or above urinals.
- **Vending cart umbrellas**—advertising on umbrellas that cover vending carts in metro markets.
- **Golf course hospitality carts**—signage on the sides and backs of hospitality carts on nearly 1,000 golf courses.
- **Dogs**—(that's right, dogs) wearing advertising messages, called K9 Billboards, are available to stroll through cities nationwide.

- **Campus laundry rooms**—acrylic-covered, framed poster-size ads are available on more than 300 college campuses and in a total of 3,500 laundry rooms.
- **Diaper-changing stations**—called Baby Boards, carry advertising in public restrooms.
- **Health clubs, spas, and salons**—ads in a variety of shapes and sizes are located throughout the facilities.
- **Public tennis courts and swimming pools**—ads on scoreboards, walls, and even on the bottoms of the pools.
- **Stadium and arena food carriers**—logos are imprinted on snack packs used to carry food and beverages.

With so many place-based media options available, choosing the right one can be tricky. Last tax season, I received an e-mail with a question from an accountant trying to build his new practice. He couldn't understand why his marketing wasn't working, yet his tactics were poorly chosen—and one in particular was really out of left field. He said he was advertising on the backs of supermarket receipts. Now, really, would you choose an unknown person to handle your finances from an ad on the back of a shopping receipt? It's a great tactic, but it was absolutely wrong for him.

Results of Choosing the Right Place-Based Opportunities

Using the right place-based opportunities should enable you to accomplish at least one or more of the following five things:

1. **Influence a purchase.** Ideally you want to find placed-based media that reach your prospects when they're in a position to buy what you sell. The last time you visited your dentist, did you notice the brochures in the waiting room promoting the tooth-whitening products your dentist applies? These "informational" brochures are excellent placed-based selling tools because they prompt patients to ask the dentist for the product or procedure.

Ads placed in and around supermarkets, for example, are effective for products sold there. In addition to ads on shopping cart returns, advertisers can place their product names or logos on supermarket clocks, buy shopping cart ads, and a variety of displays—all to reach consumers just prior to a purchase decision. Ads on cash register receipts entice customers to come back for special promotions or discounts on products they may never have tried. They can also be used to draw shoppers to stores located adjacent to the supermarket. Where will your customers be when they're deciding to buy what you sell?

2. Reach your best prospects. The most exciting characteristic of placed-based media is that they can go wherever your best prospects do. Trying to reach boaters? Ads and informational materials placed at marinas may do the trick. Are your prospects sports enthusiasts? From high school and college stadiums through professional arenas, there are countless placed-based opportunities to send your message.

Suppose you were marketing to college students. After all, 15 million college students in the United States spend more than $100 billion each year for everything from clothing and shoes to cars and electronics. On-campus advertising includes outdoor posters and dioramas; indoor posters in laundry rooms, dorms, and student unions; plus a new form of advertising available on about 100 campuses—large plasma screens that alternate ads with announcements in the lobbies of student unions and in recreational facilities. If you were a retailer marketing to a nearby campus, you could run on-screen ads 11 times per hour, sometimes 24 hours a day, 7 days a week, to promote student discounts, host on-campus promotions, and recruit employees.

3. Put your message in the right context. Place-based media often can be used to reach prospects when they're in just the right state of mind. For the same reason that business marketers advertise copiers, computers, and cellular phones using outdoor media that reach commuters on their way to work, other less traditional media can accomplish a similar goal by presenting your message in the appropriate context. If you're a member of a major health club, for example, you've probably noticed the video screens and other advertising featuring products related to fitness, health, diet, and beauty. When would you be more receptive to an ad for a new diet plan, at dinnertime while eating pizza and watching TV, or when you were working off those extra calories the next morning at the gym?

Pet owners stocking up at the neighborhood pet store are in the right frame of mind to take a brochure for a local pet groomer from a countertop rack while waiting at the register. And teenage boys playing basketball on a urban court are likely to take notice of a nearby poster advertising sports apparel. These placed-based media work because they reach qualified prospects in the proper context.

4. Appear in a compatible venue. Most people are familiar with the small posters that are placed in restaurants and clubs, generally inside the restrooms or nearby, perhaps in a hallway where patrons must wait in line. Ever notice the kind of advertising they carry? The majority is for compatible, entertainment-oriented products and services that match the "fun" state of mind of the patrons who view it. Place-based ads feature local attractions, musical events, gambling junkets, skydiving and snorkeling trips (in Miami), ghost tours (in New Orleans), and dating services, just to name a few.

Your place-based advertising should be a synergistic part of your overall marketing campaign and carry similar themes. So it's important to choose out-of-home venues that are compatible with the overall tone and content of your company's message. An ad for the tax preparer I mentioned earlier, for instance, probably wouldn't work on a nightclub restroom poster, even if patrons of the club matched the demographics of his target audience. His message simply wouldn't be compatible with the tone of the venue.

5. Earn community goodwill. Other, more subtle forms of place-based media can effectively boost your company image as a good citizen of the community. One such example is the Adopt-a-Highway program, which posts signage along major highways from coast-to-coast in exchange for sponsors' fees to cover routine maintenance. The Adopt a Highway Maintenance Corporation is one of the leading providers of the service and signage. Primarily used for branding purposes, the signage designs are approved by state highway departments, which typically allow a company name and logo. You can buy the signage along a major route close to your office or anywhere you like. In some states, signage is available every mile and in others its every two miles, and on average, each sign is seen by drivers and passengers in five million cars a month. It's a great way to show your customers and your entire community that you care.

#27 CREATE YOUR OWN PLACE-BASED OPPORTUNITIES

Even with the seemingly endless number of established place-based media choices available, you may find that you want to create your own. Do you remember Constantine Pergantis, president of Nite Lites, from Chapter 4? You'll recall he donated 4 days of work to put up 50 championship banners in the gym of the local high school. But he also created his own long term place-based media opportunity by gaining the school's permission to hang his company banner in the gymnasium—in perpetuity. That's right, now all the students and their families who attend the games in the gym will see his company name there.

There are countless ways to create your own place-based advertising. It just takes some imagination and a willingness to partner with other types of businesses. Often, these unique arrangements require no direct outlay of cash but instead only a willingness to share in the proceeds. In some instances, a commission is warranted, while in others, a revenue share agreement can be established. Here are some ideas that should help get you thinking:

An upscale kitchen remodeler approaches the owners of an appliance showroom concerning joint promotion. Because the retail showroom has no design and installation capability, it sometimes loses customers who are looking for a more turnkey approach to upgrading their kitchens. The result: The remodeler creates a short video showing newly completed kitchens that runs on a continuous loop on a video monitor in the showroom. It's accompanied by signage and brochures that detail the "new service."

A baker specializing in wedding cakes has no retail outlet, so she contacts a local bridal shop concerning a place-based promotion. The bridal shop is looking for an additional revenue stream, and the baker agrees to pay a commission on all cakes sold as a result of the promotion. The result: The baker places a beautiful wedding cake display (specially created so it can remain in place for a long period) in one of the store's windows. The promotional materials include a rack brochure and a photo portfolio, resembling a wedding album, showing available cake styles for store personnel to share with interested customers.

A dog trainer wants to reach new dog owners by placing signage in local, independently owned pet shops. The result: He creates and distributes a poster with puppy housebreaking tips. It includes an adorable Dalmatian puppy and a fun headline, "Spots look good on him, not your carpet." The poster shows six tips for housebreaking, and the trainer's company name, logo, and phone number appear prominently at the bottom.

As you can see, sometimes it's possible to put your promotional media in place without any direct cost other than creation of the materials themselves. Mark Sussman, president of Dance Distributors, likes a smart marketing challenge. He's the Harrisburg, Pennsylvania–based small-business owner I introduced you to in Chapter 2. A third-generation entrepreneur, he's also earned an MBA in marketing and has come up with some brilliant ways to increase his company's reach. Even though Dance Distributors mails hundreds of thousands of catalogs a year (in addition to conducting an extensive online campaign), Sussman's ongoing mission is to increase the size of his company's mailing list in order to win new customers.

With that goal in mind, Sussman advertised in *Dance Teacher Magazine* and then rented the publication's mailing list. His goal was to create a poster that dance teachers would want to put up in their studios and that would give students a strong reason to respond. He came up with the idea of sending an attractive poster with an attached tablet of business reply cards. The cards offered a chance to win a $50 gift certificate simply by registering to receive Dance Distributors' free catalogs. All a student had to do was tear off a card, fill it out, and send it in. As you can imagine, Sussman's place-based advertising promotion generated thousands of new names for his company's mailing list, and he effectively turned every dance studio that displayed his poster into a free advertising venue.

You can choose to use any of the thousands of available out-of-home and place-based media opportunities, or you can even create your own. With a little ingenuity, you can put your message in front of your best customers—even if you're on the tightest budget.

6

SAVE WHILE
GOING POSTAL

There are two effective ways to use postal mail to build your business. How does your company use it? Do you send direct mail to open doors for customer acquisition? Or perhaps you create sales letters to follow up leads and telephone contacts. With the ideas in this chapter, you'll find it's possible to do both and still stay on budget.

Direct mail is a terrific tool—if you know how to use it properly. The term *direct mail* typically describes a large mailing that may consist of a postcard, letter, dimensional-mail package (such as a tube or box), or catalog. Successful letter mailings follow specific copy and design formulas based on years of testing and the experience of marketers nationwide. So you can expect to see a typical letter mailing that contains:

- A carrier envelope imprinted with a teaser
- A cover letter that includes a Johnson box (a line or two of copy in a box-shaped outline or tinted box highlighting the key message of the offer) at the top, a special offer or hook,

copy that details the benefits and outlines the offer, a signature in a second color, and a postscript
- Product inserts or coupons
- A business reply card and envelope

Letter mailings are sent in large quantities—generally, a minimum of 5,000 pieces—because the typical positive response rate is between 2 percent and 3 percent. The execution process includes copywriting and designing the creative pieces, choosing and renting the lists, and delivering them along with the creative to a mailing house for labeling and distribution. As you can guess, this is rarely a low-cost or do-it-yourself process.

There are small businesses such as Dance Distributors, which mails 350,000 catalogs a year, that rely on direct mail for a significant percentage of sales. And other businesses that routinely send mass mailings of letters. But for the majority of small-business owners whose sales are not driven by mail order, there are lower-cost alternatives to expensive mass mailings that deliver high returns when used for customer acquisition. Let's start with a money-saving idea for business-to-business marketers.

#28 MAKE AN IMPACT WITH DIMENSIONAL MAIL

If you want to ensure your message gets noticed, put it in a box. Unlike flat mail, which is often discarded unopened, dimensional mail piques everyone's curiosity. In 2004, dimensional mail averaged the highest overall response rate, at 5.49 percent, of any direct-response medium according to the Direct Marketing Association's "2004 Response Rate Report."[1] That's versus 2.73 percent for flat mail. Used skillfully, dimensional-marketing results can go significantly higher—the study noted three campaigns for "eating and drinking establishments" that averaged a response rate of 15.67 percent.

Major businesses with deep pockets often use dimensional mail to reach thousands of consumers. Small-business owners, on the other hand, can benefit from adopting this tactic to target small groups of highly qualified business prospects for less money than launching a major direct-mail letter campaign.

Remember Jeff Porro, PhD, from Chapter 2? The principal of Porro Associates in Washington, D.C., he writes op-eds, speeches, and press material for PR firms, nonprofits, and other corporate clients. Banking on the fact that his best prospects are overworked and overstressed, Porro developed a clever box mailing. In a sharp-looking, black, corrugated eight-inch cube, he placed two items—an inflatable neck pillow and a candle—both wrapped in red tissue and bearing his company logo. Also inside was a black label with a red border and white type with the headline "Your Cure for Messaging Stress." A one-page insert was humorously designed and illustrated to resemble the safety instruction sheet you review before takeoff on an airline. It began, "The perfect remedy for messages that miss the mark, prose lacking punch, and excess deadlines." Five illustrated, tongue-in-cheek steps followed:

1. Inflate pillow.
2. Call (number) to set up a meeting with Porro Associates, LLC
3. Light candle
4. Kick back and relax
5. Blissfully enjoy results from potent copy and persuasive materials

The bottom-line message was that Porro Associates would relieve the stress prospects go through when trying to communicate the right message and help them execute their work more easily and effectively. This humorous dimensional promotion was eye-catching and clever, and demonstrated the wit and intelligence behind Porro's writing work. The neck pillow and candle with his logo also had real-life usefulness, which ensured that prospects would keep them around long after the mailing.

Because Porro had a short, well-qualified prospect list, he created 150 of these kits. To generate maximum results, he sent them in groups of 20 to 25 at a time so that he could follow up almost immediately by phone. His prospects in the Washington, D.C., area received their boxes by hand delivery, and kits were mailed to prospects in New York City. Along the way, Porro received coaching from me on the initial concept and guidance on the execution of the campaign, help from a design firm to carry out his vision, and from an outside vendor who supplied the specialty items with his logo. In all, Porro spent about $3,000. As a result, he says the dimensional mailing "put me on the radar screens" of top prospects at the large PR and grassroots firms. It immediately began opening doors. After the first group of 20 kits went out, Porro set up three meetings and two major projects with new clients. The remaining 125 kits were delivered and mailed over time, every month or so, with each batch garnering at least one meeting and a number of enthusiastic phone calls and e-mails.

Following on the heels of this success, Porro has integrated other mailings, including cleverly designed oversize postcards and brochures, into his campaign. You'll remember from Chapter 2 that he also sends a successful e-newsletter and e-mail solicitations to prospects. Porro has found this is an indispensable way to stay top-of-mind and it has propelled his company to a higher level of success, with sales of several hundred thousand dollars annually.

Tips When Launching a Dimensional-Mail Campaign

Keep these five tips in mind when you initiate your own dimensional-mail program:

1. **Use a small, prequalified list.** The per-unit cost for dimensional mail is high when compared to flat mail, so it's best to send your boxed mailings to just your most important prospects. How many top, business-to-business prospects does your business

have? Perhaps there are as few as 30 or 50 in total. When you keep the number low, you can afford to spend more on the items included in your box.

Prequalification is essential to success. Your boxes must be mailed or delivered to exactly the individuals who can make buying decisions. It may take multiple phone calls to each company on your prospect list before you hit on the name of the right person, and you may choose to send your dimensional mail exclusively to prospects with whom you've had prequalifying phone calls.

2. Focus on your central marketing theme. Every marketing promotion you undertake must relate to your company's central marketing message, and your dimensional-mail campaign is no exception. Not only should your concept and execution be clever and exciting, but they must also drive home your most important marketing theme and motivate prospects to take action. What will your prospects gain by working with you? Use your dimensional mail to reinforce that primary benefit in a way that's memorable and fun.

3. Put the right items in the box. It's best to stay away from clichéd specialty items that prospects will have in abundance. Resist the temptation to send a coffee mug with your logo and the tired headline, "Wake up your sales with Jones Company." Instead, look for something relatively unique your prospects will actually want to keep. You can bet that no one in the past had sent Porro's prospects a neck pillow. Not only was it something they would want to use, but because it was imprinted with Porro's logo, prospects were sure to remember him every time they did.

4. Follow up immediately. For maximum results, mail or deliver your dimensional kit in small quantities so that you can comfortably follow up by phone in one to three business days. This step is essential. After all, the primary reason for sending the kit is to get the attention of your best prospects and to open the door for communication. An effective dimensional-mail campaign will warm up prospects and make them more receptive to your phone call—allowing you to achieve your goal of moving them further along in the sales process. And your follow-up phone call is essential to take them to the next level.

5. Make it part of an integrated program. Most business-to-business sales are not closed following one marketing or sales contact. It takes many contacts with prospects over time. So make a big impact with dimensional mail and support it with other sales and marketing efforts.

#29 REDUCE COSTS WITH MARRIAGE MAIL

If you're targeting consumers and looking for an alternative to high-cost traditional direct mail, consider marriage mail. Here's a great example of a small-business owner who uses this low-cost tactic.

Mike Pratt, vice president and owner of Lafayette Tire and Service in Lafayette, Louisiana, says he has to be cautious with his advertising dollars. But with 60 competitors in his town alone, it's hard to stand out. So Pratt's focus is on excellent customer service, quality work, and a well-targeted consumer marketing campaign.

Lafayette Tire and Service was opened by Pratt's father 27 years ago and continues in its thriving downtown retail location today with 11 employees and projected 2005 sales of $1.2 million. Though he worked in the business as a teenager and eventually went into sales there in the late 1980s, Pratt left to spend six years in the Navy before rejoining the company in 1995. A few years back, when Pratt ran a "ladies' day" oil change special, it became so popular he decided to make every day ladies' day—and now women are his primary target market. He says, "If a woman feels comfortable about where she's doing business, she's going to tell a lot of people."

By far, Lafayette Tire and Service benefits most from an ongoing marriage-mail campaign. You're probably familiar with marriage mail and have received it over the years. It brings together coupons from a variety of advertisers and mails them in a single envelope. While numerous companies provide marriage mail in cities nationwide, the preeminent provider is Valpak, which designs, prints, and mails 18 billion ads in 500 million envelopes each year that reach 46 million addresses in the United States, Canada, and Puerto Rico. An affordable alternative to stand-alone direct mail, marriage mail is used by local advertisers from restaurants, dry cleaners, clothing stores, and auto repair shops to a full range of service providers to cost-effectively target specific neighborhoods.

When Pratt found creating his own direct mail for Lafayette Tire and Service was costly and involved too much time-consuming effort, he switched to marriage mail. Now his coupon goes out in the same mailing with a landscape nursery, furniture store, clothing store, specialty shops, and prominent businesses in his town. Targeting his prospects by ZIP code, Pratt has sent 30,000 Valpak coupons a month at a cost of $795 for the past eight months. About 60 percent of his costs are covered by co-op dollars. Pratt says his bright yellow and royal blue coupons make his money back "and then some."

Originally, Pratt was planning to use Valpak only in slow months and make a superlow-price offer on oil changes, but he decided to raise the price of the offer a bit in order to offer the coupon continuously. That was a smart decision and he's found that the low-price oil change drives people in and they return for other services. The marriage-mail campaign has yielded the "highest return on investment I've ever seen . . . 80 percent are new customers," says Pratt.

Marriage mail can be an excellent way to reach consumer households in targeted neighborhoods with your company's special offer without the effort and costs associated with hiring a designer, copywriter, printer, and mailing house, and selecting and paying for rental lists. Unlike traditional direct mail, which carries your offer alone, with marriage mail you may not have exclusivity in your product or service area. The offer you develop must effectively tempt consumers. It works best for businesses in price-competitive arenas and is ideal for attracting first-time customers. Marriage mail is a sales generator, not a lead-generation tool, so you can expect to see your customers with your coupon in hand. As a result, programs are easy to track and you can effectively measure ROI.

Once your marriage-mail campaign yields a sale, it's up to you to retain that customer and keep her coming back for more. Lafayette Tire and Service puts extra effort into the environment where customers will spend time waiting. It has a lobby with cable TV and women's magazines as well as a play area and fish tank for children. There's a coffee room and a "very clean bathroom" for women. And here's an interesting customer service idea: The company also provides a private office with a desk, telephone, and calculator for businesspeople who may be waiting for their cars. Repeat customers feel so at home there, Pratt says, that he sometimes finds them sitting in *his* chair.

#30 WRITE A GREAT SALES LETTER

Postal mail is an essential channel for following up leads generated by marketing communications or sales calls, and sales letters are among the most popular tools in a small-business owner's arsenal. You can write and send them at little or no cost. And it seems there's always the need for a good sales letter—whether it's to follow up a phone conversation, a meeting, or a lead generated from marketing communications. However, because most small-business owners are not professional writers, sales letters can be challenging. It's easy to go overboard and make your letter too hard sell or, on the flip side, produce a letter with "no teeth" that doesn't present your company in the right light or move your prospect closer to making a buying decision.

Some people think writing a sales letter should be quick and simple, so they get frustrated after a short time and either give up or settle for a letter that's simply mediocre. In reality, even the best professional writers expect to spend considerable time crafting an effective letter. But that doesn't mean every time you send out a letter you should spend hours creating it. Instead, it's important to have a group of polished sales letters on hand that can be easily modified to fit specific situations.

Tips for Writing a Great Sales Letter

You can write a terrific sales letter. Start by taking a look at these six guidelines:

Tip #1. Personalize your letter. Sales letters, though coming from your business, should always remain personal in nature. They should address the recipient by name and demonstrate how your company or product will meet his or her unique needs. Because the vast majority of sales letters are sent to follow up a previous connection, you should have sufficient information to thoroughly customize your "form" letter. Be careful with the salutation. Unless you've held a conversation with your prospect that puts you on a first-name basis, it's best to adhere to a formal salutation using the recipient's last name.

Tip #2. Focus on benefits. To be effective, your sales letter must focus on the benefits the reader will gain from engaging your services or buying your products. You'll remember from the introduction to this book that benefits always answer the prospect's question, "What's in it for me?" And you'll see in the following sample letters that the benefits—or what the prospect will gain—are always contained in the first paragraph of a good sales letter. Features, the characteristics of your company, its products or services, are used in the body of your letter to explain the benefits you promise. Then it's best to restate your primary benefit in the final paragraph.

Tip #3. Make your letter outer-directed. Resist the temptation to write about what "we offer" and instead focus on what "you'll get." Do you see the difference? No one wants to read a litany of what you do, how you do it, or what you provide. They *do* want to read about how what you do will make their lives or work easier or better. So all sales letters must be written from this perspective, eliminating most uses of the words "we" and "I," and replacing them with "you."

Tip #4. Take responsibility for the next step. Smart marketers know it's a mistake to expect prospects to take action on their own. Even with a strong call to action that contains an incentive, you should still retain control by telling your prospect what you plan to do next. In other words, give the prospect the opportunity to contact you, but don't expect it. Always state exactly what action you plan to take and be sure to follow through.

Tip #5. Include a postscript. This is one sales tactic that can be borrowed successfully from direct mail, although it's not appropriate for every type of business. It's often helpful to include a postscript because recipients tend to read the salutation, then skip to your P.S. before reading the body of your letter. So put your primary benefit or any special offer in your P.S. to motivate prospects to spend time with your letter.

Tip #6. Keep it clean. Of course, I'm referring to your letter layout and design. In fact, you don't need to do anything special at all in the way of design. Just keep it simple and professional, avoiding "loud" graphics, borders, and colors—unless they're already a part of your product or brand image (because you're selling children's games or surfboards, for example). Your letter's appearance must be consistent with professional one-to-one correspondence since anything over the top may scream "junk mail." Use your business stationery and make judicious use of color and bullet styles. Avoid using many exclamation points, and stay away from copy written in all capital letters because it's actually harder to read and seems to scream at the reader.

Now that you've had an overview of the guidelines, let's take a look at some sample letters. You'll note they're relatively concise. While it's not absolutely essential to keep your letter to one page, it's preferable because prospects may set a longer letter aside until they have time to read it at length, then forget to come back to it. However, if you need more space to tell an engaging story—such as with a fund-raising letter—prospects may stay with you so long as you follow the other guidelines for a successful, outer-directed, benefit-oriented letter.

Here are four letters (see Figures 6.1 through 6.4) I've written providing examples of how to sell a consumer product, consumer service, business product, and business service.

FIGURE 6.1 *Sample Letter for Selling a Consumer Product: Sunroom Addition*

Dear Ms. Gaines:

Thank you for your response to our ad in the *Washingtonian* magazine. A [brand name] sunroom is a great way to add beauty and value to your home without the long months of remodeling required for a brick-and-mortar room addition. And you'll find it quickly becomes everyone's favorite room in the house.

With a [brand name] sunroom you can:

- Create any type of room addition. Want to enclose a patio or create a luxurious bathroom or spa? You can add a comfortable family room, a dining room for elegant dinner parties, or gaze up at the stars from the master suite you've always wanted.
- Enjoy nature in total comfort year-round. Whether you take delight in looking out at the snow on a winter's day or on a sunny

(continued)

FIGURE 6.1 *Sample Letter for Selling a Consumer Product, continued*

summer scene, you'll always have beautiful views from your new sunroom.

- Keep your energy bills in check. Only [brand name] sunrooms have our own patented glass designed to achieve the highest energy efficiency. Our new glazing technology keeps the temperature in your sunroom constant, no matter the temperature outside.
- Choose your favorite architectural style. With three styles to choose from, your [brand name] sunroom addition will enhance the beauty of your home inside and out. Because a [brand name] sunroom may be installed in a matter of weeks, you'll enjoy your new addition faster than you would with other types of construction.

You'll find more information on creating a beautiful new room addition in the catalog I've enclosed. As your local [brand name] dealer, we'll work with you every step of the way, from choosing the right sunroom to fit the style of your home through complete installation, and provide you with a full manufacturer's warranty. I'll telephone you soon to set up an appointment to visit your home and provide a written proposal. If you'd like to reach me in the meantime, please call my office or my mobile number, 000-000-0000. Together, we'll create a beautiful [brand name] sunroom addition that will add to the value of your home.

Sincerely,

Kim T. Gordon
President

P.S. A [brand name] sunroom lets you enjoy nature in total comfort year-round. Plus, installation is fast, so you can quickly enclose a patio in time for summer or add that special room you've always wanted.

FIGURE 6.2 *Sample Letter for Selling a Consumer Service: Children's Day Care*

Dear Mr. Ramirez:

It was a pleasure speaking with you this morning concerning your son, Michael. Here at [name] day school, we'll make it fun for Michael to learn all the skills he'll need to make a smooth transition into first grade. Your son will also benefit from a safe and nurturing environment, thanks to a staff of highly accredited teachers and a secure facility.

We're often asked what sets [name] day school apart from other day care providers. First, this is a happy, fun place and Michael will enjoy coming here. We use directed-play techniques designed to help your child develop skills that will prepare him to start school. Teachers and staff experience ongoing training, and we keep class size small, so every child gets individual and group attention. We also know security is an important issue, and provide electronic check-in and checkout for parents and others who are authorized to pick up a child.

Parents like you who take an active role in their children's development stay involved via regular, written reports from the teachers. And here's something unique—we welcome drop-in visits by parents, and encourage you to come by any time to participate in daily activities.

I know you're eager to get Michael started, so I've enclosed a brochure and letters of reference from parents as well as an application. You can also download additional copies from our Web site, [URL]. As we discussed, our next step is for you and your wife to bring Michael in for a meeting and tour. We've set aside an appointment for you next Wednesday, [date], at 5:30 PM, and will call you on Tuesday to confirm. If you would prefer another date or time, please let me know by phone or by e-mail at [e-mail address], and we'll be happy to accommodate you. I'm looking forward to meeting Michael and helping him to develop the skills he needs to make a successful start in life.

Sincerely,

Kim T. Gordon
Principal

FIGURE 6.3 *Sample Letter for Selling a Business Product: Telephone Systems*

Dear Bill:

Thank you for taking time from your busy schedule today to discuss your company's phone system and the daily challenges it poses for your expanding staff. A fully featured telephone system that's accurately scaled to fit the needs of your growing business will help you increase staff productivity while presenting a polished, professional image to callers.

Working together, we'll integrate advanced telecommunications technology with important telephony applications to ensure that you have a reliable, easy-to-use system that fits your budget. Features including voice mail, interactive voice response, follow-me call forwarding, multiparty conferencing, and VOIP (voice-over Internet protocol) will enable your staff to more efficiently manage customer communications and offer superior service.

You'll get a highly advanced telephone system and expert installation plus:

- Staff training. We'll educate your personnel on the new system, providing complete instructions and clear documentation regarding use of your equipment.
- Little downtime. We work hard to minimize disruption of your business. When needed, we'll install after-hours or on weekends.
- On-site follow-up. On day one with your new system, we'll be available in your offices to ensure a smooth transition.

As promised, I've enclosed spec sheets describing the advanced telecommunications systems we provide and a Needs Analysis Checklist, a quick form that will provide insight into the system features your company needs most. You can also learn more about our products and installation services on our Web site, [URL]. I think you'll find our company provides added value, including long-term maintenance contracts with special discounts on services for moves and additions, so you can be assured of maximum reliability as your company continues to grow.

I'll telephone you soon to set up a complimentary consultation to further assess your needs and provide an in-depth proposal, and you can reach me on my mobile phone [number] or by e-mail at [address].

(continued)

FIGURE 6.3 *Sample Letter for Selling a Business Product, continued*

Working together, we'll design a system that will enhance productivity and customer service—and stay within your budget.

Sincerely,

Kim T. Gordon
President

P.S. A complimentary consultation to assess your current system and challenges is our important first step to increasing the productivity of your growing staff, so remember to fax your Needs Analysis Checklist to [fax number].

FIGURE 6.4 *Sample Letter for Selling a Business Service: Medical Billing*

Dear Jennifer:

It was a pleasure speaking with you today about your group's billing and collection methods and how our firm can successfully support your efforts. Did you know that the typical medical practice loses thousands of dollars each year due to untimely filing and inexperienced or overworked staff? As the office manager of a large medical group practice, you know that billing processes can require extensive staff time and costly software, which add to your overhead and detract from the time your staff might otherwise spend caring for patients. By outsourcing your billing to [name], your practice will save money while improving your cash flow and reducing overhead expenses.

Here at [name], we use electronic claims processing to ensure you get paid in as little as 14 to 21 days. As specialists in medical billing and collection since 1990, we'll collect your aged accounts receivable and process all your claims for a lower cost than adding on-staff specialists. And because we stay up-to-date on all insurance programs, you'll get

(continued)

FIGURE 6.4   *Sample Letter for Selling a Business Service, continued*

---

the maximum reimbursement possible. We can receive your batches daily, three times a week, weekly, or monthly as you prefer.

You and the physicians in your practice can expect high-level reporting and secure recordkeeping. You'll have remote access to your reports, data, and patient records via a secure connection 24 hours a day. [Name] is HIPAA-compliant and a member of the American Academy of Professional Coders.

This information kit includes six sets of materials—one for you and each of the physicians in your group practice. Each set includes an informational brochure and letters of reference from other area physicians who are benefiting by outsourcing their billing and collection to our firm. You can also learn more about us by visiting our Web site, [URL].

As we discussed, our next step is a short group presentation that will demonstrate how easy it is to save money and improve your cash flow by outsourcing to [name]. I'll telephone you soon to set a date, and feel free to reach me anytime in my office or on my mobile number, [number].

Sincerely,

Kim T. Gordon
President

As you can see, a great sales letter presents the benefits of your products or services and explains them with features. Plus, a good letter always strives to move the prospect further along in the sales cycle by stating clearly what the next step must be. Whether your goal is a one-to-one meeting, group sales presentation, or the opportunity to present a cost proposal, close for it in your letter and then follow through as promised.

7

INCREASE SALES WITH RELATIONSHIP MARKETING

A couple of years ago, the hottest phrase on every marketer's lips was "customer relationship management," or CRM. There were books, articles, and seminars on precisely how to set up a CRM program. But as it turns out, CRM is a lot tougher than it appears. One noted industry expert reportedly said that trying to manage customer relationships is akin to herding cats. That's because customer relationship management isn't really about one thing or program—it's about *everything*—or at least every contact your company has with an individual from well before a sale takes place to long after.

Each of us has countless relationships, some more important than others. And the ones we value most are with people we trust and companies we can count on to deliver products and services that meet or exceed our expectations. How would your customers or clients characterize their relationships with your company? For many businesses, good customer or client relationships are paramount for generating positive word of mouth and referrals. For others, customer rewards or "loyalty" programs can keep hundreds or thousands of customers coming back for more.

#31 CREATE REFERRAL RELATIONSHIPS

For a great example of a company that's entirely focused on customer relationships, we can look at Bike Friday. Founded in 1992 by brothers Alan and Hanz Scholz, Bike Friday (the better-known name for Green Gear Cycling) is a family-owned business in Eugene, Oregon, that with just 27 employees successfully sells to an enthusiastic customer base throughout the United States and as far away as Japan and Australia. What does it sell? A custom-made, folding bicycle that fits in a suitcase and sells for between $1,800 and $2,200. The company describes the custom-folding Bike Friday as "the travel bike that rides like a full-size performance bike."

Think of the Bike Friday folks as the supreme masters of customer relationships. For the people at Bike Friday, success doesn't hinge on a single referral "program"—though referrals are how the company has attained much of its growth. To them it's about everything they do to connect with and support their customers. This philosophy permeates the entire organization and reaps substantial, measurable rewards. About 40 percent of the company's annual sales ($3.5 million in 2005) are from repeat customers or referrals.

Bike Friday has a factory with a showroom where customers can visit, take a tour, and test-drive bikes. But only 3 percent of its customers ever visit. The company also has a comprehensive, customer-focused Web site, yet no orders can be placed online. Ninety-seven percent of Bike Friday's sales are by telephone. According to Hanna Scholz (daughter of founder Alan Scholz), Bike Friday provides a fully customized product, so the company needs to talk to each customer and match the customer with the options he or she requires. Scholz, who is now marketing director, has been in the family business since middle school and as a teenager sewed the fabric "socks" that go over the wheels when a bike is placed in a suitcase.

The one-to-one relationship with each and every customer begins with that first phone call. Phone "interviews," as Scholz calls them, are 45 minutes to 1½ hours long. Customers are asked how and where they'll use their new bikes. (Will they want to take fast day rides or are they planning a full tour of Alaska? Will they be taking rides transporting children or with other family members, for example?) Following each initial interview, a Bike Friday salesperson e-mails a bike design to the customer. When the customer approves the design, the salesperson obtains the rider's height and weight, processes the purchase, sets up a "promise" date, and puts the custom-bike order into production. New owners receive a "Welcome to Bike Friday" packet that contains a letter and a video showing exactly how the bike folds and fits into a suitcase.

The welcome packet also includes unique referral cards. "Our customers travel all over the world and get asked about our bikes," says Scholz. So Bike Friday provides referral cards printed with each customer's name and ID number. If a Bike Friday owner is out on a ride or talking with an interested person, he can fill out a referral card with the referral prospect's name and contact information and mail it to Bike Friday. Because the enthusiastic Bike Friday owners take responsibility for mailing the cards, the company receives between 10 and 30 referral cards a month.

Bike Friday salespeople follow up every referral and the company maintains a database with customer files in which it records each referral a customer generates. When a referral prospect buys a bike, the Bike Friday owner who sent in the card can choose to receive either a $50 check or a $75 credit toward bike parts or another bike. Select bike dealers in local communities in the United States and abroad also refer prospects and receive $100 if a prospect buys. Current Bike Friday owners even receive a self-referral reward when they buy another bike.

"One customer, Margaret Day, has organized a Bike Friday tour in Australia," explains Scholz, who says Day is 70 years old and "has just gotten her second $3,000 bike free." That's because Day just can't resist spreading the word about Bike Friday. While the company's typical customer is between 45 and 65 years old, with an average age of about 55, Scholz describes many as retired yet extremely active. Some Bike Friday Club members recently spent two months riding across Alaska. "The customer joins a community and we appreciate them as part of the community," says Scholz "and we help to maintain that community by keeping them up-to-date, sharing interesting stories with them, and listening to their feedback."

Relationship marketing is so important at Bike Friday, it actually has a "company evangelist" on staff. Australian Lynette Chiang is a customer turned employee whose focus is on connecting bike owners to one another and to the brand. A former advertising copywriter, she purchased a Bike Friday in 1996 to travel through numerous countries. In 2000, Chiang published her book, *The Handsomest Man in Cuba,* about her three-month-long travels through Cuba on a Bike Friday. And by 2001, Bike Friday's owners persuaded her to join the company and move to Eugene.

Take a look at some of the ways Chiang, Scholz, and other Bike Friday employees build customer relationships through the Bike Friday community:

- The Bike Friday Web site (BikeFriday.com) is a fun, informal site dedicated to its users. There are links to product information and the latest catalogs, but for the most part the site showcases Bike Friday owners and allows them an opportunity to share their stories and interact. Customers' own photos are featured on the home page. Under the "community" tab, there are pages with an events calendar, Bike Friday clubs, customer reviews, referral awards, a "What do you do on a Bike Friday" section, the YAK discussion board, and Web club.
- Approximately 8,000 customers receive a monthly e-mail from Bike Friday with a travel story featuring a customer. E-mails

encourage customers to send pictures and stories for the Bike Friday Web site. Communications are informal, friendly, one-to-one. Says Chiang, "I think that our personality comes through in everything we write, so it sounds like we're sitting right there talking with you over a chai latte."

- Unpaid endorsements from celebrities and industry experts also build word of mouth and lead to referrals. According to Chiang, six-time Race Across America champion Lon Haldeman and Tour de France commentator Phil Liggett are Bike Friday owners. So are key industry personnel, including former *Bicycling* editors Frank Matheny and Ed Pavelka, and League of American Bicyclists director, Preston Tyree.

- Chiang reads the YAK discussion list daily and says hundreds of customers share information and occasionally problems. She works to correct the problems and often sends gift certificates to complaining customers—as a reward for sharing their opinions. The company considers this feedback invaluable as this helps it find out about problems and come up with good ideas for new bikes.

- Bike Friday Clubs are what Chiang calls "self-perpetuating loyalty centers out in the field." Free for anyone who wants to ride their bikes regardless of the manufacturer, these clubs are organized and maintained entirely by volunteers and supported by Bike Friday. When a club leader decides on a ride, Bike Friday e-mails contacts in its database within a 60-mile radius of the starting point, encouraging people to join the club's online message board. Bike Friday provides club jerseys free to club leaders and at a discount to all riders. Says Chiang, "Everyone wins because they get a social activity, create a formidable public presence, people visiting the area can look up a club and go ride with them, people who want to test-ride bikes have a ready group to consult, referral rewards are generated, and best of all it's free advertising for Bike Friday."

Bike Friday Club events help the company extend its customer relationships into communities nationwide and even into other countries. And for every individual relationship they create, Bike Friday opens doors to countless referral opportunities.

But what if you don't have a fun product like Bike Friday that customers can experience through test-rides? Other kinds of customercentric events can be used to reward customers or clients and win referral business. In the financial products and services industry, for example, client appreciation events and educational forums can be used to generate referral prospects just by encouraging guests to bring referrals along with them.

Low-key, client appreciation events can combine a thank-you lunch or after-work hors d'oeuvres with an informal talk on a subject, such as retirement planning. Or you can host roundtable dinners and ask your best clients to invite people who may be interested in the subject matter. If you're targeting seniors, however, events held earlier in the day work best. By keeping your group small, you'll encourage attendees to ask questions and increase the amount of time you can spend with each client and referral prospect.

#32 MARKET TO "INFLUENTIALS" AND "INFLUENCERS"

If you're serious about creating a successful, low-cost campaign to build referrals for your growing business, then you should consider adding a marketing campaign to reach at least one of these two groups: influentials or influencers.

Influentials

Influentials are consumers who are instrumental in advising and recommending brands and products to their friends.

According to market research company NOP World, influentials are twice as likely to recommend products and services and also twice as likely to be sought out for their advice. You know who these folks are—they're the ones with connections to large networks of friends and who always know which is the newest *in* place or style, or they're "experts" about certain types of products, such as new electronics. Depending on your type of business and who your key influentials may be, you can develop a campaign to reach them that includes special invitations to events, e-mail announcements and exclusive offers, online PR placements (such as on product review sites), and placements on targeted blogs.

Influencers

Influencers are often businesspeople who have direct contact with your prospects.

Real estate agents, for example, exert significant influence over which mortgage brokers new homebuyers select. CPAs and bookkeepers also influence their clients when it comes to selecting financial planners and investment consultants. Are your business prospects influenced by other business owners or professionals? If so, developing a business-to-business marketing program to target influencers should be your top priority. Consider your influencers a primary target audience and create a campaign to reach them. But don't duplicate the campaign you use to reach prospective customers or clients. Focus on the benefits you provide to influencers and create marketing messages that motivate them to think of your company as a qualified, capable, and trustworthy referral resource.

#33 LEARN THE STEPS
TO WINNING REFERRALS

For some businesses, a full-blown marketing campaign to reach referral sources may be overkill, while for others it's just a first step.

Ten Low-Cost Ways to Obtain Referrals

If this growth strategy is important to you, here are ten more low-cost ways you can win referrals for your business:

1. Ask the right people. Your current customers or clients can't send you referrals if they don't know you're looking for them. It may sound simplistic, but it's essential to directly communicate with your customer or client base that you are open to referrals. It's also important to let them know the kinds of referrals you're looking for. After all, some may not be fully aware of the scope of your company's abilities or services.

You can ask verbally or put your referral request in writing. Suppose you were a consultant working with a division of a major corporation. You could ask your client if there are other divisions in his company that might be able to use your services and, furthermore, to make the introductions to key executives. Your client could set up three-way phone conversations to introduce you or simply call and lay the groundwork. Or suppose you were a remodeling contractor. At the completion of each project, you might supply the homeowners with a satisfaction survey and, at the end, ask for names of other homeowners who might be interested in remodeling. You could also ask select homeowners to write testimonial letters.

2. Create interpersonal relationships. For many small-business owners, referrals hinge on creating relationships with influencers. The bottom line is people refer business to others they know and trust, and this is an instance in which it's necessary to combine sales with marketing tactics to produce the results you need. The first step is to make a list of influencers and contact them by phone to set up appointments to get acquainted. You can invite them to lunch or simply coffee, so long as you schedule an opportunity to sit down in a professional context and learn about each other's companies. It's important to discover under what circumstances they would be open to sharing referrals, and to determine how you can help them meet the needs of their customers or clients. Once you have initiated a relationship, keep in touch and be patient—it may take a while to instill the confidence necessary to generate business.

3. Send handwritten notes. So many entrepreneurs swear by this tactic that it's impossible to ignore. Emily Sanders, president of Sanders Financial Management, Inc., in Norcross, Georgia, is a highly successful networker who says she and her colleagues often send handwritten notes to contacts and associates. Though her time for marketing is limited, Sanders has built a thriving business that grows 25 percent a year and believes this tactic is well worth the effort.

You can send notes as thank-yous, to acknowledge someone else's achievements, or to simply follow up with someone you've recently met. The key is to make the note personal and solely about the recipient. It's not an opportunity to write about your business or its services, though you should always tuck in a business card. Use attractive stationery, and be sure to hand address the envelope and apply a real stamp (instead of using a postage meter). This will be consistent with the personal tone of your note and help ensure it gets past screeners.

4. Track referral sources. It's vital to show your appreciation to referral sources, but that's impossible to do if you don't know precisely where your referrals are coming from. That's why it's essential to train everyone who answers incoming calls to ask prospects where they heard about your company. Then you can track this information in your marketing database. When you receive a referral from a known source, promptly send a thank-you letter or handwritten note to express your appreciation. Referral sources who send you significant business warrant additional attention and thanks, such as a special luncheon or gift (where appropriate).

Tracking the sources of your referrals will also give you important information concerning the types of businesses or individuals that are more likely to send work your way. You can use this information to refine your referral marketing program to target additional influencers who fit the same profile.

5. Use public relations. Referrals, like trust, are earned over time, so it's necessary to establish your company's credibility with potential referral sources. One of the best ways to accomplish this is through public relations. Place stories in key media both online and off-line that your referral prospects look to for quality industry or professional information. Once you do get PR coverage, send copies to the referral prospects in your database. If you're using postal mail, attach a brief, handwritten note. And if you're sending a copy of your coverage by e-mail, avoid a hard-sell approach by leading in with a simple note introducing the piece (pasted below and not sent as an attachment) as an item of special interest.

Another option is to create a company newsletter with case histories. This soft-sell approach should demonstrate to your targeted referral prospects that you are solving problems for your customers or clients competently and professionally.

6. Expand your Web site. Your Web site is often the first place people look when they want to learn more about your company and what it offers. That's why it's important to modify the site to meet the needs of either influentials or influencers. If you sell a product whose sales can be affected by what key influentials say, then give them lots to talk about. You can supply expert or customer-driven product reviews, or follow the example of BikeFriday.com and feature customers' stories, and add a blog or a discussion group.

To motivate influencers to send referrals your way, consider adding a separate section of your Web site just for them. They shouldn't have to wade through lots of content that's directed to the end user (customers or clients). Add a link from your main toolbar to pages that directly answer their questions, and let them know how to contact you.

7. Provide specialized tools. Do your principal influencers meet or work directly with your best prospects? If so, it's a smart idea to supply them with marketing tools they can use one-on-one with your targeted prospects. Anything from brochures, handy guides, and "tips" sheets that will be given away to your prospects should be imprinted with your company name and logo. This will position your business as a valuable resource and ensure your company name or message reaches your ideal prospects.

It's likely that these tools and materials are already being supplied by your principal competitors, so take time to evaluate how you can make yours the most effective and useful. You don't want to produce a lot of materials that will end up unused. Discuss with your influencers exactly what kinds of tools and materials they would like to receive and tailor your tools to meet their specific needs.

8. Offer incentives. I offer this tip with a major caveat attached. In some industries it may be appropriate to provide financial rewards for referrals. If this is the norm in your industry (and is legal and proper), you may wish to consider offering financial incentives. Just take care that you don't trumpet rewards for referrals in the same space in which you ask customers or clients for their business. This can actually backfire by weakening your company's credibility and the effectiveness of your marketing campaign. In short, it can just plain turn off your end users.

9. Communicate frequently. Staying top-of-mind is just as important when communicating with referral audiences as it is with your prospective customers and clients. "Touch" your referral prospects at least once every four to six weeks using a combination of sales and marketing tactics. For example, you might start by communicating with a telephone call, follow that with a meeting, a hand-written note, e-mail your company newsletter, make contact by phone, send an article or other materials by postal mail with a brief note, arrange a visit to your referral prospect's office, and so on. Get the idea? By alternating sales with marketing and by sending only materials that you know will be of special interest to your referral prospects, you'll create an effective program that builds referrals over time.

10. Instill trust. The real title for this tip should be "Don't blow it." Customers or clients who come to you by referral must be treated with the utmost care. In most instances, they're highly qualified and motivated. Chances are, they're already thinking about purchasing the types of products or services your company offers, and the only thing left to do is to convince them to buy *from you.* Also, every action you take from the time a referred prospect contacts your company through long after the sale is closed will be judged as "pass or fail" by the person who made the referral. After all, the way you handle the referral will reflect positively or negatively on the referrer. One of the cardinal rules of successful referral relationships is to always keep those who send you referrals up-to-date on the outcome. If you do a terrific job with the referrals you receive, you're bound to earn more.

#34 MOTIVATE CUSTOMERS WITH REWARDS

There's a good reason why customer rewards programs are often called "loyalty" programs. It's because they do a stellar job of keeping customers loyal to you—not your competitors. And in price-sensitive arenas and where there are parity products and services, securing customer loyalty may mean the difference between successfully building your business and struggling to stay afloat. An effective customer rewards program can increase sales while lowering your marketing costs. After all, it's considerably more pricey to run campaigns to woo new customers than to keep existing ones in the fold. In fact, it can cost as much as five times more to win a new customer than to retain an old one.

Customer rewards programs are so pervasive among large businesses that about half of all Americans belong to at least one. Grocery stores, credit card companies, and major retailers all offer rewards to stimulate repeat sales. For example, drugstore chain CVS Corporation supposedly has signed more than 32 million "ExtraCare" card members alone.

Like big businesses, small-business owners are embracing loyalty programs as a way to retain customers and stay one step ahead of the competition. Stanley's Tavern in Wilmington, Delaware, is a prime example. Established in 1935, it's been under the ownership of Steve Torpey for the past 23 years. *Delaware Today* magazine has named it either "Best Bar and Grill," "Best Neighborhood Restaurant," or "Best Sports Bar" every year for the past 20 years, though Torpey describes it as more of an American-style, family-oriented restaurant that's "filled with kids all the time" than a bar. Ribs and a 66-item salad bar are Stanley's Tavern specialties. There are also more than 40 television screens, Monday Night Football promotions, and something for all major sporting events including basketball, baseball, even World Cup soccer. But what makes Stanley's Tavern unique is the relationship that the owner and the entire staff have with customers. "Restaurants are the cornerstone of the community," says Torpey. "They're where you celebrate birthdays and engagements," and building a community of loyal customers is what has allowed Stanley's Tavern to excel above a vast sea of well-heeled competitors.

According to Torpey, 20 years ago Bennigan's was the only major chain restaurant within 6 or 7 miles of Stanley's Tavern. Now, there are about 20, and they're predominantly proven chains such as the Olive Garden, Red Lobster, TGI Friday's, Lone Star, Outback Steakhouse, and Ruby Tuesday's. If that weren't enough, there are also about 8 local chains in the area. Despite this intense competition, Stanley's Tavern has projected 2005 sales of more than $3 million.

About ten years ago, when Torpey saw the immense buildup of new competitors in his market area, he decided to create a loyalty program that would touch all his customers, not just the core regulars he knew. It took a while to set up, but by the summer of 1997 his customer rewards program was in place. Today, it's called the Frequent Fan Club and has 5,400 members who earn a point for every dollar they spend on food and beverages, banquets, and gift certificates, plus special rewards points for other things, such as answering survey questions.

When a new customer comes in, a waitress asks if he's aware of the Frequent Fan Club and leaves an application on the table. The customer fills out a three-by-five card with his e-mail address, name, birthday, address, and phone number, and then receives a membership card. Every 400 points earns a customer a $10 restaurant certificate, and if he earns all 400 points in a month, he gets an extra $5. In 2004, Stanley's Tavern gave away $36,000 in customer rewards—and since 1997, $200,000 worth of earned coupons have been issued.

In the beginning, the only problem with Torpey's program was that it cost him an arm and a leg to administer it. Just mailing out earned coupons ran $10,000 a year. Then in August of 2004, he transitioned from postal to e-mail rewards when he began using LoyaltyTrak software from Smart Button of Newark, Delaware. LoyaltyTrak is a Web-based loyalty solution that costs Torpey $1 a year per enrolled member (reducing his costs to $5,400 per year), plus it allows him to analyze the frequency and spending habits of his customers using information that's managed and stored using the software.

Torpey also purchased a kiosk from Smart Button for his lobby. Customers use the kiosk to check their points and can immediately print out coupons to use in the restaurant. The lobby kiosk allows Torpey to give random rewards as premiums. Naturally, this encourages customers to use the system and participate in the Frequent Fan Club. Every fifth person to swipe her card, for example, may receive extra points, or Torpey can decide to give rewards to everyone who comes in from two to five in the afternoon. For added convenience, customers can check their rewards on Stanley's Tavern Web site, http://www.stanleystavern.com.

The top 10 percent of Stanley's Tavern customers, about 50 people, have received a Gold Club card. This gives them reservation privileges—a major benefit in a restaurant that's almost always busy. There's also a Travel Club. About four or five times a year, Torpey negotiates great prices for groups to go on Mediterranean cruises, or trips to Nassau, Mexico, or the Dominican Republic. According to Torpey, twice he's had enough people to fill an entire aircraft. This is relationship marketing at its best.

In addition, these group trips have given Torpey a bargaining chip when it comes to negotiating special rewards for Stanley's Tavern customers. "We've given away 20 Caribbean vacations for 2 over the past 7 years," says Torpey. This is thanks to a joint promotion with Apple Vacations, which donates trips in exchange for promotion in the restaurant.

Beyond a top-notch loyalty program, there are at least three more ways that Stanley's Tavern builds special relationships with customers. First is what Torpey calls "the Cheers factor, where everybody knows your name." He has trained his staff to look for the top 100 customers and says that when customers come in they may hear their names five times before they even get to their tables. This has also helped build employee retention because staffers feel a part of the Stanley's Tavern family. One-third of the staff has put in more than ten years of service.

Then there are the golf tournaments and live sports broadcasts. Over the past 11 years, Torpey has raised $550,000 for the Boys and Girls Clubs in Delaware by organizing an annual celebrity golf tournament. And on Monday nights, radio broadcasts from Stanley's Tavern on an AM talk station feature predominantly high school sports. The local coaches and teams come into Stanley's Tavern to talk live on the air. "We may have a 15-year-old high school player who just won local lacrosse player of the year come in and bring his family," says Torpey.

In the restaurant industry, and in many others as well, 23 years of success means you're a superstar. Clearly, Steve Torpey's customers agree.

#35 SET UP YOUR OWN
LOYALTY PROGRAM

Are you ready to develop a loyalty program to retain customers and increase sales for your small business? Follow these seven tips for developing a loyalty program that will produce the results you need:

1. **Construct your database.** Your first step is to enroll your customer base in your new loyalty program. Because it's much less expensive to manage your rewards program online than to use postal mail, capturing e-mail addresses is vital. If you have a Web site, you can add a box to your main page and offer an incentive for enrollment as well as enroll customers at checkout. Brick-and-mortar retailers can place a special promotion at the registers and enroll customers waiting in line to make purchases.

Stephen Marder, PhD, of Duluth, Minnesota, is the co-owner of Golden Oak Stables, an online business specializing exclusively in the sale of Breyer collectible toy horses. Marder, who was formerly director of the Center for Economic Development of the University of Minnesota at Duluth, stumbled into this business by accident when he put his grown daughter's Breyer horse up for sale on eBay. He found that 5,000 to 10,000 Breyer horses are sold on eBay at any one time. Naturally, this discovery sparked the interest of this small-business development expert, and Marder founded the company with his wife, Joan, in July of 2003. Now less than 5 percent of their business comes from eBay, and Marder has built an enrolled list of 7,000 customers called "Stable Friends." GoldenOakStables.com is an enormous success, and in 2005 Marder projects sales close to $1 million.

2. **Motivate your customers.** Your enrolled members will be more likely to participate in your program if they know exactly what rewards they can expect to earn. Programs that balance immediate gratification with long-term benefits are the most effective. Con-

sider how the Frequent Fan Club members at Stanley's Tavern are immediately rewarded for answering a survey question on the lobby kiosk while checking the number of points they've attained toward their long-term goal of 400. It's unwise to exclusively use the element of surprise when it comes to rewards. Customers who have nothing specific to strive for are less likely to participate in such programs.

3. Offer graduated rewards. For many types of businesses, the majority of customers tend to purchase a group of core products and rarely venture to others that are new or have higher price points. By offering graduated rewards, you can encourage first-time sales of these items. For maximum participation, make your rewards easy to obtain, then as customers step up or receive larger rewards for bigger purchases, you can tempt them to apply their rewards to sales of bigger-ticket items that they might otherwise consider out of reach. When you offer graduated rewards, you also avoid the problems inherent in programs that reward primarily on enrollment, which attract low-value "price switchers" who go from one program to another, taking advantage of first-time buyer rewards.

Programs that feature high-value rewards, such as discounts or points accumulation for rewards, can be costly. So it's a good idea to alternate with intangible rewards for members only. For example, the top earning members of Stanley's Tavern Frequent Fan Club become Gold Card members and receive an additional, less tangible reward—special reservation privileges. This balance of high- and low-cost rewards can reduce your overall financial outlay while keeping customers satisfied.

4. Provide in-kind rewards. One of the most important reasons to institute a loyalty program is to create a positive, ongoing relationship between your customers and your company. Which would be more likely to reinforce a positive experience with your company, brand, products, or services—rewards that your customers can obtain only from you, or unrelated rewards, such as movie tickets or coupons to a nearby ice-cream parlor? The answer is simple. To be successful, your loyalty program should offer in-kind rewards that bring your customers back to you.

5. Stay top-of-mind. The 7,000 Stable Friends of GoldenOakStables .com receive loyalty program e-mail every four to six weeks with new product announcements and advance notice of new limited editions. Unlike many other types of solicitations, permission-based e-mail with information about customer rewards is not only acceptable, it's desired by many purchasers and leads to repeat sales. In DoubleClick's 2004 consumer e-mail study, nearly half of the consumers surveyed expressed an interest in receiving information about membership rewards programs, and about three-quarters have redeemed online coupons for purchases.[1] You can also keep customers up-to-date by postal mail; however, it will be more costly.

6. Gather customer data and feedback. Another bonus of instituting a customer loyalty program is the invaluable data you'll amass. Data collection is at the heart of these programs. While the bulk of the information is gathered when customers enroll, important data is gained later by monitoring transactions and through surveys and polls. By monitoring transactions, Steve Torpey's program tracks everything each customer orders, allowing him to create special rewards solely for the segment of people who order dessert, for instance.

Over time, your competitors will come and go and customer perceptions will shift. That's why it's essential to continually survey customers and solicit their feedback. Torpey awards additional points for Club members who answer brief survey questions, such as "What publication do you look in when you decide to go out?" This helps him modify his advertising program.

7. Measure performance. To ensure the success of your loyalty program, you must monitor more than its ROI. Fine-tuning and adjustments must be made based on important customer information. You'll want to know:

- How often customers buy
- What they buy
- How much they spend per transaction and per year
- The time between purchases
- The number of customers who join and the percentage who lapse

For example, Stephen Marder knows that 35 percent of Golden Oak Stables's business is to repeat customers. The average sale is $70. Sixty percent of the company's sales occur in November and December, but some customers order every month. This critical information informs all aspects of his business decisions from advertising to staffing.

You can achieve the same level of success as the businesses in this chapter, from Golden Oak Stables to Bike Friday and Stanley's Tavern, by setting strong goals for your own company's customer relationship programs. Whether you institute a referral campaign to spread the word via influencers and influentials, or create a hardworking customer rewards program, you'll transform your company through solid relationship marketing.

8

TEAM FOR DOLLARS

In competitive sports, *team play* often means one side clobbers the heck out of the other—and the winners take all. When it comes to business, you'll still find business owners and so-called experts who believe that for someone to win, somebody else has to lose. Fortunately, for many highly successful and ethically content small-business owners, that kind of thinking is too last century.

Success rests on building alliances that serve all parties, whether you're forming friendly ties with the competition, partnering with other businesses for marketing, or coming together through networking functions. Teaming can extend your company's marketing reach and give you access to more prospects and clients or customers. Partnering can lend you the expertise to offer additional services to your customer base, or put the power of larger partners behind you. And in many cases, teaming with other businesses can make your marketing dollars go farther or even reduce your marketing costs.

#36 FORGE COMPETITIVE ALLIANCES

Researchers have found that the most successful entrepreneurs focus on maximizing profits or increasing their company's value, not trampling the competition. "You learn very quickly you can't do it all by yourself," says Marianne D'Eugenio, owner of Quadrille Quilting in North Haven, Connecticut. A former hospital finance director who also tried her hand at consulting, D'Eugenio never intended to start a quilting shop, though she had been quilting as a hobby for many years. But when she took a course through the Small Business Administration on starting a business, she had to write a business plan on something and thought it would be a fun idea to explore.

Eight months later, in November of 2002, D'Eugenio opened her shop with fabrics from England, Japan, and Indonesia and quilting patterns purchased from local New Englanders. Situated close to Yale University, Quadrille Quilting gets visitors from all over the world who are pleased to return home and say they got a pattern from Connecticut. Quilting classes are also a major asset to Quadrille Quilting's bottom line, and D'Eugenio has about 25 teachers that come in and give instruction in different techniques. According to D'Eugenio, she doesn't compete with the chain stores because of the high quality and price points of her product mix. This is an important point of differentiation and a contributing factor in the shop's success.

Just weeks after opening her store, D'Eugenio says she was surprised by a call from Marty Childs, her closest competitor and the owner of a shop just 15 minutes away in Cheshire, and soon they formed an alliance for marketing along with seven other shops. Childs invited D'Eugenio to participate in a "Shop Hop" in October of 2003. This was a consumer promotion organized by nine retail stores—consumers bought a "passport" and visited the shops to get their passports stamped, win prizes, and enjoy refreshments. An enormous success, the Shop Hop sent 400 people to D'Eugenio's store in the four days.

After another Shop Hop with all nine stores in September of 2004, D'Eugenio, Childs, and one more nearby competitor decided to organize their own events. The first was on Super Bowl weekend, 2005, and in those two days, D'Eugenio says she did a month's worth of sales. This three-shop event was less expensive to host because the trio decided not to incur the outside advertising costs they had with the larger group and each of the three shop owners promoted the event in their newsletters. D'Eugenio uses direct mail and has more than 1,000 customers on her list. She hopes to transition to e-mail to reduce her costs, but is waiting to see what success her competitor, Childs, has with it first.

Why would D'Eugenio want to share her customers with her two closest competitors? Because she benefits from the traffic sent to her by the other shop owners. "Customers are getting to see what other shops sell, and mine is very different from the other two." D'Eugenio specializes in floral patterns, the shop in Cheshire focuses on Asian motifs, and the third shop, in Durham, features pastels. Most important, the Shop Hops help bring in people for D'Eugenio's classes, which are promoted in her customer newsletter. A crush of new customers comes through the door during the Shop Hops and the staff asks them if they have Quadrille Quilting's newsletter. If not, they quickly sign them up. During the last Shop Hop, D'Eugenio brought in eight employees for each of the two days, double the number she employs the rest of the year.

D'Eugenio says she benefits by having someone to "bounce ideas off," and she and Childs compare information on marketing strategies as well as team for the Shop Hops. The bottom line is that this competitive alliance is helping Quadrille Quilting increase its sales 20 percent year over year.

Benefits from Forging Competitive Alliances

As you can see, at least half a dozen benefits can result from forging competitive alliances. Try these on for size:

1. Reach new prospects and customers. Like D'Eugenio, alliances can help you reach an entirely new customer base. These new prospects are extremely well qualified because they already have demonstrated their interest in the type of product or service you sell. As a result, they're more likely to have a shorter sales cycle and require little education in what you market.

2. Gain important information. Going it alone can lead to lots of trial and error when it comes to marketing. But a competitive alliance or even an association of friendly competitors provides a forum for sharing information that can save you from making big mistakes and guide you toward what has proven to be effective for others. In short, you'll learn from your competitors' successes and failures.

3. Get more bang for your marketing buck. By joining together for promotion, your marketing dollars will go farther. Consider how the three quilting shop owners each promoted the Shop Hops in their newsletters, effectively giving their individual shops three times the reach without spending a penny more. In addition, forming a competitive alliance for advertising, for example, can provide funding required to conduct a larger multimedia campaign.

4. Acquire purchasing or distribution power. Some friendly competitors form associations or co-ops. In addition to marketing as a group, you can benefit by joining forces to purchase larger quantities of materials at reduced costs or to share distribution channels. Forming a co-op may give you more clout and save you money.

5. Raise awareness as a group. You're probably familiar with the advertising campaign for Florida's Natural premium orange juice, which comes from a "co-op of growers." Approximately 1,100 individual growers belong to a co-op owned by 12 companies, all pulling together to create a nationwide campaign with considerable impact. This is in the face of their primary competitors in the juice business, which are owned to a great extent by large soft drink companies.

Here's another example. Suppose you owned a high-technology company in an area not necessarily known as a high-tech mecca. You might band together with other technology companies to market as a group, thereby raising awareness of your presence in the region and enhancing the image of all.

6. Create a national presence. It can be challenging to operate a single-unit small business with one office that's facing down national competitors. Why not form your own nationwide network of like-minded businesses? A financial services firm in Minneapolis might become affiliated with others in Chicago, Tampa, Atlanta, San Francisco, Dallas, and Phoenix, for example. They could share common business practices, strategies, and philosophies while retaining individual ownership, yet present themselves as a strong, nationally affiliated group.

#37 EXPAND YOUR BUSINESS WITH PARTNERSHIP MARKETING

Almost everyone has seen major businesses promote their "partners"—other businesses they've joined with for marketing purposes. Nowadays, these are rarely partnerships in the old sense of the word, where joint ownership of a business was involved. Look at Entrepreneur Media, for instance. My firm is a partner with Entrepreneur.com, the magazine's Web site, to market our coaching services. *Entrepreneur* magazine is a partner with America Online and they share my magazine column with AOL to run on AOL.com. Many large and small businesses assemble such partnerships and benefit from becoming marketing partners. With all this linking up, you wonder how any company can afford to go it alone these days.

Partner to Create a Whole New Product or Service

Just ask Valerie Young, owner of Changing Course in Montague, Massachusetts. Founded in 1995, her business started out offering a subscriber newsletter. Soon she advanced to selling online subscriptions and eventually transformed her business by offering her e-newsletter free and selling additional products and services, including e-books compiled from the newsletters. The newsletters often included articles from well-known writers, including Barbara Sher, author of *I Could Do Anything If I Only Knew What It Was,* and Barbara Winter, author of *Making a Living without a Job.*

Young, an experienced trainer and workshop leader who once worked in strategic marketing at a Fortune 500 company, decided to approach Sher and Winter about a marketing partnership. Her idea was to partner to provide a four-day workshop retreat for women and then market a CD kit produced from tapes of the event.

Young had to assemble a lot of pieces, and she carried the weight of much of the costs associated with creating and promoting these products. The event, called "Making Dreams Happen," involved a $30,000 investment—costs for the taping, production of giveaway bags, a workbook, copywriting for the promotion on the Web site, and a brochure Young created for the three partners to use to promote the event. Young spent another $15,000 developing the CD product, which ended up including 23 audio CDs and a pdf of the workbook.

In all, Young is reimbursed through the revenues generated and all three partners split the profits. The three each promote the CD set on their own Web sites, and when a purchase is made, customers click through to a shopping cart on Young's site. "The partnership has produced financial benefits and it's nice to have colleagues that share your world," says Young, who is pleased with her company's projected sales figure of $225,000 in 2005.

Since the first workshop, Young has teamed again with Winter and British author Nick Williams for a workshop entitled "Dreams Can't Wait." And in the summer of 2005, she and Winter are partnering to offer "Turning Passions into Profits." However, their financial model has changed. Rather than charge between $1,300 and $1,700 per attendee, now the fee is set at around $200 for early registration. Young says she'd rather have 150 people who can arrange for their own food and lodging than organize a small group at a pricey mountain retreat, and she has decided not to create all the expensive giveaways.

Young's marketing partnerships continue to evolve and she has no worries about joining forces to create mutually beneficial products with individuals with whom she might otherwise compete. In her view, "It's a big world and there's plenty for everyone."

Partner to Acquire Customer Rewards

Remember Steve Torpey from Stanley's Tavern? He's given away 20 Caribbean vacations for two over the past seven years as special rewards to his customers. But instead of spending a fortune, Torpey partners with Apple Vacations (a major vacation package broker) through a local travel agency, All About Cruises and Travel, as well as product suppliers such as Budweiser.

The trips are provided in exchange for marketing promotion in the restaurant, such as a link to the travel agency's Web site from the Travel Club page on the Stanley's Tavern site. As for Budweiser, during football season each "Budweiser dollar" a customer spends earns him a point, and the person who buys the most wins a Caribbean vacation for two paid for by Budweiser. Torpey says it's not uncommon to have a customer order a round of Budweiser for the entire bar in order to increase his chances of winning. And it's a big bar.

Partner to Reach a Larger Market

You've already seen how a small business such as Quadrille Quilting can partner to extend its marketing reach. In that case,

D'Eugenio is partnering with her competitors, but you can also partner with small businesses that provide complementary services to provide a well-rounded offering that appeals to a wider target audience.

Suppose you were a remodeling contractor and you wanted to increase the percentage of your business that came from high-end bathroom remodels. You could partner with a bath and plumbing fixture showroom and offer a turnkey service, from design and fixture sales through completely remodeled baths. For marketing tools, you might supply a rack brochure to display in the showroom or coproduce a video featuring beautifully remodeled spa-like baths with decorator tile and fixtures to run continuously on a display monitor. Of course, you'd also promote the partnership in a joint ad campaign and train all the showroom staff to promote your full-service partnership.

It's increasingly common for small businesses to become marketing partners with major companies or associations. In other words, they become what are called "affinity partners." Everyone is familiar with affinity programs, though you may not have previously heard the term. If you have a major credit card, chances are you've been pitched to use the services of the provider's partners, from rental car companies to prepaid legal services. That's an affinity program in action.

When you partner with a major marketer, you gain several strong advantages. First, you have access to its immense customer base and you may be invited to include your marketing offers in mailings or other solicitations from your larger partner. Next, you have the advantage of working with a partner that's experienced and knowledgeable at marketing to the target group, so you won't waste any effort or make an off-target pitch. And, finally, you'll save the tens of thousands of dollars you might have spent going after the target audience (the customer base of your larger partner) on your own.

Most affinity programs or other marketing partnerships are known to operate smoothly, but if a more in-depth partnership or funding is involved—such as when a small company has new technology and joins with another company to comarket it—legal protection is essential. Copyrights and patents are important, yet a full patent application can cost $10,000. So consider a provisional patent, a preliminary step that gives you 12 months of protection and often costs less than $1,000 in attorney's time. Another way to protect yourself is to ask your potential partner to sign a short agreement up front. Don't hesitate about asking for this kind of protection, which is commonplace when two Fortune 500 companies are joint venturing. Also, as a necessary precaution, take time to research your potential partner's legal cases, partnerships, and joint ventures for any red flags.

Partner for Powerful Endorsements

What could possibly be the basis for a partnership between a company marketing to girls ages 9 to 12 and Charles Schwab, head of (well, you know) the huge, national investment company? A healthier message built around the challenge of dyslexia. Let's start at the beginning . . .

Addie Swartz is the CEO of B*tween Productions, based in Lexington, Massachusetts. While her company name may not ring a bell, chances are if you have a daughter or are close with a girl between the ages of 9 and 12 you've heard of Swartz's products— the books and merchandise that create the world of the Beacon Street Girls. At this writing, 180,000 Beacon Street Girls books have been printed since September of 2004, and they're sold nationwide in major stores, including Barnes & Noble and Borders.

"We're all about doing good for girls," says Swartz. "We offer a place for girls that's healthy, realistic, and normal. Not blonde, thin, and rich." Swartz is successfully building a brand that includes the books and a range of branded products that appeal to girls who are at the age between toys and boys. Her characters have been carefully developed with extensive input from her target audience (lots more about this in the next chapter), and they deal with real-life issues. One of the Beacon Street Girls, Maeve, is dyslexic, and so are Charles Schwab and his son.

Schwab Learning, part of the Charles and Helen Schwab Foundation, has created the Web site SparkTop.org ("where no two brains spark alike") for children challenged by dyslexia. A promotional partnership with the Beacon Street Girls is an ideal fit and Swartz offers contests on SparkTop.org, including a "Meet Maeve" sweepstakes in which 100 site members won "stylin' stuff from the Beacon Street Girls." In April and May of 2005, they ran a sweepstakes called "My Big BSG Adventure Sweepstakes," giving children a chance to get their name in Book 6.

Partnerships like this one generate sales by adding liberal doses of word of mouth. It can be hard to go cold into a major company to pitch a partnership. And developing relationships with larger partners can take time. But if you can find a special connection—whether it's a challenge in common, such as dyslexia, or a special benefit you can deliver to your potential partner's target audience—you'll have a much greater chance of success.

#38 MAKE NETWORKING PAY

Networking may be a form of sales, but it's the softest sell around. Successful networking isn't about going to the most meetings and shaking the greatest number of hands. It's about working closely with select individuals and organizations. That's teamwork and it pays off in new friendships and, often, clients.

Successful networking also has a lot to do with passion. Just ask Emily Sanders, president of Sanders Financial Management, Inc., in Norcross, Georgia. A financial planning and portfolio management firm with $100 million under management, this small business boasts revenue growth of 25 percent year-over-year using primarily networking and public relations tactics. The company's target audience is composed primarily of women, or what Sanders describes as the "emerging affluent investor." Sanders Financial Management has just over 100 clients in the United States and abroad, and with seven on staff, a low client-to-staff ratio that allows it to offer customized services. So the firm is looking for the right clients who are a good fit, but not a vast number, allowing Sanders to be selective about how she allocates her networking time.

Sanders's advice on networking success is to "do something you love." She participates in women's organizations, does community service, volunteers, and gets involved with university alumni organizations, as well as attends events sponsored by business magazines, religious organizations (synagogues, churches, community centers), as well as political fundraisers where she and her business partner meet affluent women who are donors. This may sound like a lot, but Sanders likes to pick and choose and limits herself to about three functions a month, while her business partner attends just one or two.

The key to Sanders's success is the highly active and visible roles she undertakes. She may give a speech or take a leadership position by heading a committee. In March of 2005, for example, Sanders flew to Paris to present a keynote speech at a women's financial conference entitled "Money Matters for Women." And every February for eight out of the past ten years, when the U.S. congressional session reopens, she and a group of about 60 Atlanta women go to Washington, D.C., to meet with congressional representatives. Sanders takes an active leadership role as head of the educational committee and helps organize the agenda as well as gives inspirational and instructional speeches to the attendees. "I enjoy all the things I do and am passionate about them. The people around me pick up on that and they want to learn more," she says.

Sanders says she wouldn't join an organization just for the sake of meeting people who could use her company's services but, she says, "if it's something I love and believe in and the people there believe in the same things I do, we strike up a conversation and perhaps they're in a position in their lives or have a friend or family member who's at a point where they can really benefit from our services." This is a basic principle of successful networking—giving time and energy to other people and organizations in order to receive.

Top 12 Pointers for Successful Networking

Contrary to what some "experts" would have you believe, networking is not meant to resemble an Olympic sport. So I'll dispense with a lot of the hard-sell tips you may have seen elsewhere and give you a rundown of my top 12 pointers for achieving superior results from your networking efforts.

1. **Choose quality over quantity.** Networking, like many sales tactics, is a low-cost way to build your business. But let's not forget that time, as they say, is money. That's why it's important to be extremely selective when it comes to choosing the organizations in which to participate. To narrow your choices, begin by making a list of the meetings and events at which you'll meet the highest percentage of members of your qualified target group (these may be prospective clients or customers, or important influencers). Then attend a few meetings to get a feel for the different organizations. From that, you'll be able to assess and narrow your list of organizations, groups, or events to the select few you wish to join.

2. **Focus your message.** Before you attend a networking function, it's important to create an introduction that will help those you meet remember what you do and how it can help them. You should be able to describe what your company does in a single sentence. Suppose you owned an IT consulting firm. It would probably be a waste of breath to introduce yourself by saying, "I'm James Doe, of Doe IT Consulting. We specialize in systems for a range of businesses." Yawn! Here's a better approach, "I'm James Doe. My company, Doe IT Consulting, helps small businesses upgrade to centralized systems to manage client information better and boost sales." What do you want people to remember about you? Make

your introduction memorable and benefit-oriented and you're guaranteed to intrigue more listeners.

3. Find areas of common interest. Whether your targeted prospects are surfing enthusiasts or investment bankers, it's smart to find venues or issues around which you can come together and serve your mutual passion. For Sanders, whose target audience is affluent women, she's able to meet her best prospects by joining organizations where women participants have similar interests to her own. Passion is communicable. When you show enthusiasm, others will want to join you, and you'll find it easy to work and bond as a team. From there, you'll establish a foundation of friendship and trust from which business relationships may grow.

4. Step outside your immediate circle. Yes, it's true. In order to network, you will have to talk to strangers. But I'm not going to insist you "work the room" or set a goal of meeting 30 people per event. Meet and greet as many individuals as feels natural and comfortable when you're standing and moving about the room. Try not to get hung up with any one person for so long you miss out on the opportunity to properly network with a sufficient number of prospects. Then, once you're seated at a table, it's only polite to introduce yourself to the people on your immediate right and left. From there, say hello to everyone at your table. Make eye contact, smile, and remember that—even if you're bit nervous—body language speaks volumes. Try to relax and focus your interest on each individual you meet, rather than letting your eyes move about the room looking for the next "conquest."

5. Ask questions. Most people hate being "sold to," particularly at anything other than a sales meeting. Even though it's important to communicate clearly what you do and how it will benefit those you meet, keep it short and sweet. It's best to stay away from delivering a "pitch" and instead focus on others. One of the best ways to get to know people is to simply ask questions and show your interest in them. If you're shy or often hesitant to meet new people, jot down a few business-oriented questions prior to the event that will get your conversation started on the appropriate track. What do you need to know to decide if someone is a prospect? Early in the course of your conversation with each individual, be sure to ask the basic questions that will help you uncover the ways you might help each other.

6. Take visible roles. Successful networking requires a lot more than just showing up. It means standing out in a crowd. When you work hard to help the group, you gain the opportunity to meet many more members and to work side by side with them toward a common goal. Follow Sanders's example and chair committees that will allow you to meet other members. Volunteer to speak at meetings and conferences or play an instrumental role in securing others to speak—and you're bound to be asked to go to the podium to introduce them. If the group has a newsletter, you can write articles. Host or help organize fund-raisers or other special events. These are just a few ways that you can be a group member others remember, know, and trust.

7. Help others achieve their goals. One of the basic principles of successful networking is that you must "give in order to receive," and you'll find that it's just plain good business to help those you meet achieve their own personal or business goals. Perhaps you can facilitate introductions, make referrals for others in the group, or assist their business associates or family members. By asking questions, working as a team, and investing time in the organizations and people you meet, you'll become an integral part of their business and professional lives. Networking is not about tit for tat, but it's been proven by effective networkers everywhere that if you work hard to help others, they'll do the same for you.

8. Ask for business cards. As you network, you'll find it's vital to collect cards for three important reasons. First, it will help you remember the names of the people you meet. For many people, it's challenging to remember names the first time they hear them, so looking at the name printed on a card helps them connect names with faces. Second, obtaining a business card will give you the information you need to follow up properly. And third, you'll have the basic data necessary for making a new entry in your database.

9. Add contacts to your database. By now, you understand how vital a customer and prospect database is to the successful management of a sales and marketing program. When you meet a qualified individual through networking, you should add his or her name to your database along with any pertinent details—these can be anything from the prospect's company or product information to her birthday or favorite hobbies. For example, networking may bring you into contact with fellow golfers, sailors, mothers-to-be, bridge players, etc. These commonalities should be noted in your database so you won't forget them. By focusing on what you have in common with your new acquaintances, you can more quickly establish rapport and build relationships.

10. Decide on a next step. Suppose you encounter a well-qualified prospect or influencer in the course of your networking. It's a smart idea to decide what your next step together will be. Can you arrange a meeting, a meal, or simply promise a phone call? Take the opportunity when you're face-to-face with your prospect to propose a next step. Just be careful not to jump the gun. Your prospect will be more anxious to agree to a meeting, for instance, if she understands all the ways it will benefit her. So it's a good idea to establish a solid rapport first and then close for the next step.

11. Follow through. In most instances, first encounters at networking functions will require some form of follow-up. For best results, take action within 24 hours by sending a handwritten note or an e-mail, or by making a follow-up phone call, whichever seems most appropriate. Once you've added the prospects you meet through networking to your database, they should receive ongoing news about your company. You may also choose to include them in solicitations, if appropriate. Alternate sales and marketing tactics to keep your relationship moving forward. For example, first you meet in person at a networking event, follow up with a handwritten note, then a phone call, a lunch date, your e-mail newsletter, a second meeting at a networking function, your e-mail newsletter, and so on.

12. Expect results to take time. Unlike placing an ad or running a special promotion, networking results take time and patience. Sanders judges her networking efforts to be successful if her firm gets one new client from a particular event or organization. But it can take six months to a year before a prospect she's met at a networking function—or someone who's been referred to her company as a result of her networking efforts—becomes a client. "You have to give things time to percolate," she says.

9

FIND THE
PERFECT NICHE

We're a nation of niche market-
ers. In fact, with the huge population of North America, it's virtually impossible for any business to achieve success without tackling
its markets niche by niche. Anything else would be impossibly costly.
Niche marketing is how a business starts, as well as how it grows.
And even this country's largest companies expand by taking on
additional market share in one niche and then moving along to
capture another.

For example, Cannon makes printers for small offices (that's
one niche) and it also makes affordable desktop machines for home
offices (another niche), and even smaller, mobile printers that
salespeople (yet a third niche) use right from the front seats of their
cars. As you can see, a niche market need not be small—and some
are quite vast. You can create a product, or product and service
bundle, specifically to appeal to a niche market, or you can take an
existing product or service and acquire new customers by marketing it to an entirely new audience niche.

By focusing on a narrow niche market, you'll have the ability to create a marketing program that reaches your best prospects plus avoid paying for wasted media exposures. You'll also save the time you might otherwise lose meeting with unqualified prospects generated by unfocused marketing efforts. The fact is, niche marketing saves you money and time while increasing sales by appealing to the prospects who are most likely to respond to your marketing messages.

#39 TARGET NICHE MARKETS

To fully demonstrate the impact and value of niche marketing, let's look at several smart small-business owners who are achieving success by plumbing niche markets.

Emily Sanders, Sanders Financial Management, Inc.

You'll remember from the last chapter that Sanders's firm, based in Norcross, Georgia, targets women nationally and internationally who are what she calls "emerging affluent investors." What's most interesting is that Sanders didn't set her sights on this niche market arbitrarily. She perceived what she believes to be a lack of quality service for members of this target group and was determined to offer the kind of service she knew they wanted.

According to Sanders, affluent women often fail to receive the proper respect and attention from male brokers who, she says, don't look them in the eye or even visit them face-to-face. "I've heard of women with a million dollars who haven't heard from their brokers in six years," she says. Another example Sanders cites is that women, when meeting with a male broker along with their husbands, are disrespected by not being given a business card. She also states that young widows, after their husbands have died and they have inherited a great deal of money, often don't get the respect from male brokers they deserve. Their calls and questions go unanswered.

Sanders is quick to point out that not all male brokers have this failing. She says her business partner, who is male, is sensitive to the needs of women clients who seek that respect. But some women simply prefer to deal with another woman. So Sanders focuses her marketing efforts on her niche market—affluent women investors—and wins more business by providing the superior service they're looking for. The result: 25 percent business growth each year.

Scott Vincent Borba and Joseph Shama, e.l.f. Cosmetics

If you think there's no new wrinkle to be explored in the cosmetics industry, you haven't heard of Scott Vincent Borba and Joey Shama, the creators of e.l.f. (Eyes. Lips. Face.) Cosmetics. This young duo (Borba is in his early 30s and Shama his early 20s) joined forces to create a high-quality, low-cost cosmetics line—so affordable that every item is priced at $1. Their target: women ages 18 to 34 who want the quality they find in products from L'Oréal and Revlon, which are often $6 to $7 per item, but at a lower price point. "You don't see anything in that lower price range for them," says Shama.

When the two met, Borba brought the experience he'd earned with Hard Candy, Shiseido, and Johnson & Johnson where he, according to Shama, "spearheaded the Neutrogena production development team for cosmetics and then moved over to Murad" (a high-end skin-care line). Shama brought funding from his family's company, trading part ownership for start-up funds. Shama and Borba then spent 18 months putting their line together. The team decided to develop a four-tone makeup line and encourage customers to mix and match. This decision came thanks to focus groups with makeup artists in New York and Los Angeles, who said that out of the 34 base shades typically available, they use only four to six at most. The packaging is designed in the United States, the product is manufactured in Asia, the packages are filled in a facility in New Jersey, and the company has offices in New York City.

Borba and Shama began selling their line in 2004. At the outset, they developed their product line specifically for dollar stores because of the projected growth in that arena. But although they put the product into regional stores, they never placed it in the large chains that would have given them the volume they required. Shama says they quickly learned that those stores and their customers were not concerned about high quality and were selling packages of lip gloss catering to young girls or value packs to older women.

This simply wasn't where he and Borba wanted to take their company. Their niche, they believed, was to create a brand that stood as an alternative to department store brands at a price point everyone could afford. In drugstores and mass stores, according to Shama, when it comes to lower-priced lines, there's been a concentration on the teen market. e.l.f. Cosmetics was determined to target women who are a bit older, though the pricing enables the company to have "tremendous spillover," Shama says.

They created a Web site (eyeslipsface.com) and began to build their own customer base. The partners used the site to help them interact with customers and discover what they were looking for and how the company could give it to them. Shama and Borba examined the problems women in that age group face on a daily basis and specifically tailored their products to meet those needs. They found, for example, women wanted an eye shadow that was noncreasing, so they created their eye shadows using corn silk. Women ages 18 to 34 were also concerned about dry, chapped lips, so the team developed therapeutic lip balm that has antioxidants that repair lips all day long. All these modifications address the needs of a more mature (nonteen) market, while still keeping their products at the $1 per item price.

A public relations program generated tremendous national press—yielding as many as 50 placements reaching all different demographics in the first year. They were featured in magazines from *O, The Oprah Magazine* and *Parenting* to *Glamour* and *Lucky.* The partners also hired Buzz Marketing Group to take trend spotters to spread the word on college campuses. And Shama and Borba changed their entire retail focus from dollar stores to mass retailers. At a trade show, they initiated a relationship with the buyer for Target and found the chain was open to bringing in a cosmetics company that was in sync with their "expect more, pay less" tagline. Now, e.l.f. Cosmetics are in Target stores and will also be in Wal-Mart in 2005. Plus, the company has international distribution in the United Kingdom, the Philippines, Australia, and Venezuela. In all, e.l.f. Cosmetics projects sales of between $5 million and $7 million in 2005.

So how did this young company get off the ground so quickly? Shama says it's because they saw a disconnect between what the media was predicting and what the stores were showing. Find a niche that isn't being catered to, he advises. "Do the retail shopping and ask yourself, What would you like to see that's not there?"

Tara O'Keeffe-Broadbent, O'Keeffe's Company

What if you have a terrific product and want to attack a new niche market but that niche doesn't even exist—*yet?* If you're Tara O'Keeffe-Broadbent, you create it. After all, she's created everything connected to her Sisters, Oregon–based business, O'Keeffe's Company, from scratch—from the formula for her product, the manufacturing process, and now a new kind of packaging and unique entry point into a major sales channel.

The daughter of a cattle rancher, O'Keeffe-Broadbent says her Irish father's skin didn't hold up to the Northern California climate and he could never find a product that would prevent his hands and feet from cracking and bleeding. She also saw that the carpenters and carpet-layers who worked with her homebuilder husband had the same problem as her father. A pharmacist, O'Keeffe-

Broadbent decided to create a product that would effectively cure the problem. With three very small children at home, she worked on the formula at night for months. Rather than use lanolin, which was in other products, she used glycerin, a humectant that, she says, draws more moisture to it, altering the pH of the skin and causing the skin to produce acid-based chemicals that contribute to the healing process. When she had her test formula ready, she tried it on her father and he noticed a difference in days.

Encouraged, O'Keefe-Broadbent gave her new cream away at the community pharmacy where she worked and people came back and asked for it over and over again. So, in 1994, she began selling O'Keeffe's Working Hands Creme predominately through feed and farm stores. Soon she landed her product in Rite Aid stores. And in 2000, when the company was doing about $500,000 in sales and had four employees, O'Keeffe-Broadbent decided to risk the $25,000 it would cost to take a booth at the national Efficient Collaborative Retail Marketing (ECRM) trade show and ended up securing a large sale from Walgreens.

Want to know how? It seems customers had written thousands of unsolicited testimonial letters. O'Keeffe-Broadbent says she knew she'd be successful if she could "get those letters in front of a buyer who'd realize that most cosmetics don't change people's lives by helping them heal their skin."

Now you probably think this is the end of the story. But it isn't at all, because soon after the Walgreens sale, O'Keeffe-Broadbent began to realize that the national drug chains just weren't where the product needed to be. "When you walk into a drugstore, our product sits among 70 to 90 other products," she says. "Our customers have tried cosmetic products and they're not what they're after." Her goal is to be "the first leading skin therapy for people who work with their hands." And that required going after an entirely new niche market—changing the company's focus from pharmacies to hardware/home-improvement stores. The trouble was, these stores didn't have an established category for her type of product, which they saw as belonging to the cosmetics industry.

But although she was initially turned away by Home Depot, she persevered.

What you have to understand about O'Keeffe-Broadbent is that she has a very strong vision of her company selling nationally and internationally. She's created her own in-house factory with the capacity to produce 10,000 jars a day using a unique "hot" manufacturing process, plus a new, award-winning package that she describes as halfway between a "chewing tobacco can and a car wax container." Specially designed to appeal to men, the distinctive jar has a low profile, is a highly visible brilliant green or blue, has a rubber grip in the rim of the lid, and a translucent top. In all, it fits neatly into a pocket or toolbox.

This package was introduced at the National Hardware Show in May of 2004 and has since won two major awards, the 2004 Cosmetic and Personal Care Package of the Year award and the coveted, international DuPont Package of the Year award in 2005. It's also bowling over buyers at the national chains, who can now see the potential of the new niche category O'Keeffe-Broadbent has created for their stores. In addition to her unique, award-winning packaging, she's created highly visible, dramatic black-and-orange shelf counter displays, six-pack display packaging, floor displays, counter rings, and hanging dispensers for her two products, O'Keeffe's Working Feet and O'Keeffe's Working Hands.

At this writing, she has a commitment from Lowe's to put the products in stores nationwide, and both Home Depot and Tractor Supply have committed to run tests in approximately 10 percent to 20 percent of their stores to see if the products sell like they believe they will and to test the various merchandising options. Today, O'Keeffe-Broadbent expects projected sales in 2005 of approximately $2 million.

No matter where you are or what you sell, there's a narrow target market that you can address or a niche category you can enter. And if you envision an opportunity, but the right niche doesn't presently exist, follow O'Keeffe-Broadbent's example and create one.

#40 SAVE WITH
MULTICULTURAL MARKETING

If you're looking for a smart, low-cost way to expand your business, consider taking on ethnic markets. With the general affordability of ethnic media and the tremendous escalation in the buying power of ethnic groups, it may be the brightest way to take your product or service to new niche markets.

Let's take a closer look at the buying power of ethnic and minority populations, including Asian-Americans, African-Americans, and Latinos. By 2008, nearly 5 percent of the U.S. population will claim Asian ancestry, according to the Selig Center for Economic Growth at the University of Georgia, when Asian buying power will reach $526 billion.[1] Asian buying power is driven by the fact that Asians are better educated than the average American and hold many top-level jobs in management or professional specialties. For dramatic growth, look at African-American buying power, which is increasing by a compound annual rate of more than 6 percent. Meanwhile, a new U.S. Census report states that 41.3 million Hispanics now reside in the United States, and the Selig Center projects Hispanic buying power ($926 billion) will exceed even that of African-Americans ($921 billion) in 2007.

Latinos are now not only the nation's fastest-growing minority group, but also its largest, accounting for one in every seven people in the United States. Latino households are more likely to be made up of couples with children under 18, and often include extended families with three wage earners. As a whole, the Latino population is young—60 percent of Latinos in the United States are younger than 28 years old. This tendency toward larger families with young children means they buy more household goods, and will drive nearly a fifth of growth in apparel and shoe sales and about one-third of the growth in food sales through the mid-2000s. Right now, Latinos spend, on average, $300 more per year on food and $250 more on apparel products and services than the general market does. So whether you're marketing anything from baby care and health and beauty products to home furnishings and entertainment, you can benefit from targeting this group.

One of the most outstanding characteristics of this market niche is Latinos' strong tendency toward higher-than-average brand loyalty, making them prized, long-term customers. Latino women, who make many of the purchasing decisions for their families, are most concerned with buying the best quality, and are not easily swayed by price point. However, a product or service representing a true improvement or technological advance will tempt this group, since sampling something new may be seen as a progressive and positive thing to do.

Even within the lower-income segments of the Hispanic market, brand name, quality, and good customer service sway the purchase more than price. One survey by Research Data Design (RDD) revealed that 85 percent are willing to pay more for quality and prefer to buy a more expensive but trusted brand rather than a less expensive but unfamiliar one.[2] The postsale customer experience is also an important selling point, as 94 percent of Latinos are likely to buy the brand that provides the best customer service. And according to the latest People en Espanol "Hispanic Opinion Tracker Survey," 56 percent of the U.S. Hispanics polled said, "I love to shop," compared with 39 percent of the general population.[3]

What makes targeting ethnic and minority markets so affordable? The high number of quality media outlets—there are more than 1,100 black-formatted radio stations around the country targeting African Americans, according to Arbitron—and the surprising cost-efficiency of ethnic media.[4] For example, the average black-and-white, full-page ethnic magazine ad may cost six to nine times less than an ad in other national magazines with smaller circulations. Cost-per-thousand (CPM) rates for ethnic radio and television stations are generally lower as well. This is true even in cases where Spanish-language stations are tops in their time periods, which often occurs in Miami, Los Angeles, and New York.

If your business is based in a market with a large ethnic population, or if you have a product or service with the right appeal, it's a smart move to add ethnic media to your mix. That's certainly been the case for the venerable Miami-based company, Farrey's Lighting and Bath. Family-owned since 1924, the company and its marketing have evolved along with this hot metro area, which has become home to a large population of Cuban-Americans and a business gateway to Latin America.

Four generations of the Farrey family have guided this business through many transitions. Founded as a small general store in 1924 by John and Emily Farrey, it was their son Francis who, during the housing boom of the 1950s, focused the company on lighting and bathroom fixtures. The next generation of the family, Bud Farrey (chairman and president) and Frank Farrey (vice president and CFO) have continued to grow the business while facing outside hardships, including the 1980 Miami riots, which temporarily wiped out the business, and Hurricane Andrew in 1992. They were joined in the 1990s by the family's fourth generation, Paige and Kevin Farrey. Today, the company has about 120 employees, two elegantly beautiful showrooms, and projected 2005 sales of $39 million, according to Vice President of Lighting Andy Gato, who has himself been with the company a remarkable 38 years.

As Miami's population and its business focus has changed, Farrey's has added marketing tactics that target Miami's Latino residents and South and Central Americans. The campaign strives to reach upscale Latinos who are either bilingual or Spanish-speaking only. The company used to export extensively to North and South America in the past five to eight years, but the political and economic situations there have changed. Now, Gato says, these Spanish-speaking customers come to the United States to buy property and need to furnish their Miami apartments or buy merchandise to take back to Latin America, and are reached by the company's ads in the Spanish-language edition of the *Miami Herald,* the *Nuevo Herald.*

Other publications Farrey's uses to target its market may reach both bilingual and Spanish-speaking-only prospects, including upscale magazine *Selecta Magazine,* interior design publication *Casa & Estilo,* and the Spanish edition of the chic *Ocean Drive* magazine.

According to Gato, when it comes to sales generated by this market niche, those he terms "bilinguals" make up 40 percent, and Spanish-speaking customers account for 15 percent to 20 percent. All customers, including those in Central and South America, also regularly receive direct mail from Farrey's.

Another important aspect of Farrey's campaign targeting the Hispanic market is its participation in functions within the Hispanic community, ranging from fashion shows to active membership in the Latin Builders Association. This well-rounded mix of tactics has created name recognition for the business over the years and now, Gato says, "We have second- and third-generation customers coming to buy from Farrey's."

Tips for Creating an Ethnic Marketing Campaign

If this success story motivates you to plan your own ethnic marketing campaign, follow these six tips:

1. Speak the right language. English-language proficiency does affect the extent to which ethnic populations rely on advertising that reaches them in their own languages. Among Latinos in particular, however, Spanish is a key marker of personal, social, and political identity. This makes Spanish-language media important even to fluent English speakers who regularly utilize other media, and advertising in Spanish is an essential component of an effective ad campaign.

A poll by Bendixen & Associates for New California Media found that 66 percent of ethnic Californians agreed that businesses that advertise in the ethnic media "seem to understand my needs and desires better than other companies," and 63 percent agreed that they are "more likely to buy a product or service advertised" in an ethnic-oriented publication or program.[5] Hispanics exhibited the strongest "advertising loyalty" characteristics, followed closely by Asian-Americans. A study by the Roslow Research Group showed commercials in Spanish were three times more persuasive among bilingual Hispanics and six times more persuasive among Spanish-dominant segments.[6] Among Hispanic teens, ads in Spanish were twice as persuasive as ads in English. Clearly, a strong reason that ethnic media often produce superior response rates is that loyal readers, viewers, or listeners appreciate receiving communication in their own languages—and support the companies that make the effort.

2. Recognize ethnic group diversity. When addressing multicultural markets, you must remember that even among Spanish speakers, regional language and cultural differences exist. Take the word *truck*, for example. West of the Mississippi, it's *troca*, and east of the Mississippi, it's *camion*. For Cubans, beans are *frijoles*, while for Puerto Ricans, they're *habichuelas*. It's also a mistake to treat Cuban, Puerto Rican, Mexican, and Central and South American immigrants alike because factors such as family size and education, as well as income levels, differ. Cubans, for instance, tend to have the smallest families and Mexicans the largest.

3. Choose media wisely. Ethnic media often carry information for and about their local communities that's virtually ignored by other press. In California, for example, where the Asian-American, African-American, and Hispanic communities make up about half the state's population, the New California Media poll showed that nearly half of these and other ethnic groups prefer to get their news and information from ethnic media outlets.[7] While major ethnic media outlets are plentiful, from *Ebony* magazine and *La Opinión* to the Telemundo television network, many Web sites also are available, plus excellent, community-based ethnic media that represent extremely cost-efficient media buys. In Charlotte, North Carolina, for example, the weekly Hispanic newspaper, *La Noticia*, is well read and involved in the community through special events. With a circulation of 30,000 in 13 counties, its advertisers are both Latino and Anglo businesses targeting the Hispanic community.

Your local ethnic radio stations may also offer real value, particularly if you're targeting Hispanic consumers. According to the Arbitron's "Power of Hispanic Consumers Study 2004–2005," Hispanic consumers listen more to the radio than read newspapers or watch television, averaging more than 22 hours per week and spending half their radio time listening to Spanish-language formats, from tropical to talk.[8]

4. Buy frequency first, then reach. As with any media buy, you must reach your core target audience and advertise with enough frequency for your message to penetrate. Don't spread your ethnic media dollars too thin by choosing many outlets. Instead, focus on the ones that seem the most central to the lives of your prospects and provide relevant content. You probably noted that Farrey's Lighting and Bath, for example, advertises in an upscale Spanish-language interior design magazine—an intelligent, well-targeted media buy. Once you've achieved sufficient frequency with your core target audience in select media outlets, you can expand your campaign by purchasing additional reach using more print, broadcast, or online media.

5. Tailor your campaign themes. For your ethnic marketing campaign to succeed, its themes must be in sync with the cultural and ethical mind-set of the targeted community. A humorous campaign targeting young Hispanics, for instance, that pokes fun at parental authority or family unity will be deeply frowned upon, even if that same campaign plays well with the general population. That's because, as a group, Hispanics have been shown to value family, religion, and the ethics of hard work to a greater degree than the general population. Before you take the plunge into ethnic media, familiarize yourself with the cultural hot buttons of your target group, and don't hesitate to ask the media for help in tailoring your initial ads.

6. Participate in the community. Ethnic marketing is a lot more than just placing ads. You must become involved in the community to build clear affiliations that translate to sales. Look for ethnic-based community festivals, committees, fund-raisers, and awards programs, and become a recognized participant or supporter.

Doris Cevallos, president of Alianza Mortgage and Alianza Realty Group, knows the value of community involvement, and her Charlotte, North Carolina, businesses are thriving. Cevallos derives 96 percent of her business from Hispanic clients and advertises in *La Noticia* as well as participates in the paper's community events.

A well-rounded set of additional activities includes sponsoring soccer pay-per-view at a large sports bar, including handing out flyers, putting up a banner, and displaying the company logo and information on the big screen during breaks. Alianza is part of the Latin American coalition and the company sponsors a booth at the group's major event, attended by 15,000 people, at the Mint Museum. Cevallos also participates in the Latin American Women's Association, and at its gala party and carnival, Alianza is featured in the event program and on the projection screen.

What's really fascinating about Cevallos's story is that she actually created her business to meet the needs of an untapped market niche. She started in the Charlotte area in real estate, and discovered it was very difficult to find people who would handle mortgages for her clients because, she says, "A lot of them don't have the money in the bank, they don't always know about credit, and a lot are bad recordkeepers." So she had a difficult time placing the mortgages and often they would fall through. That's when Cevallos started learning about the mortgage business by working as a processor and loan officer while continuing with real estate until she was ready to start Alianza Mortgage in 2001. Now the company has a total of nine on staff, including agents, and projected 2005 gross fees of $25 million, or about $1 million in income.

According to Cevallos, there has been a 600 percent growth of Hispanics in just the past decade in the Charlotte area because of job opportunities and new businesses. She was in the right place at the right time, and when she started ten years ago, the Hispanic community was just starting to arrive in the area. Today, there's a lot more competition, yet Alianza Mortgage is the only Hispanic-owned company in the area and remains the only one that focuses primarily on the Hispanic community. One of Cevallos's loan officers contributes an article each month to *La Noticia* covering topics that include refinancing, how to build and fix your credit, and, she says, "how the Hispanic community ends up paying more for mortgages." As a result of her company's positive work and efforts in the community, Cevallos was honored as the Business Woman of the Year in 2004 at *La Noticia*'s Excellente awards.

In addition to Alianza Mortgage and Alianza Realty Group's consistent ad campaign, community public relations, and networking campaign, they also send a direct-mail newsletter to clients. It's no wonder that 75 percent of their sales comes from repeat business and referrals.

#41 CONDUCT YOUR OWN CUSTOMER RESEARCH

For Cevallos, it was easy to figure out exactly what her potential customers needed and devise a strategy to provide it. For many other businesses, however, answers and clear direction are a bit harder to come by. How will you find out what your customers want, or even who your best prospects will be?

Before you take on any new market niche or revamp your product or service offering, it's vital to conduct rudimentary research. This doesn't mean you have to spend tens of thousands of dollars on mall intercept studies, national telephone surveys, or formal focus groups (although, if your budget allows, these are definitely wise tactics). For companies that are just moving beyond the bootstrapping stage, two types of research can be conducted affordably—online research and informal focus groups or roundtables composed of your target audience members.

Numerous online research firms have assembled lists of individuals who are willing to participate in surveys, and some have gathered "advisory groups" that are regularly surveyed on specific topic areas. When you hire an online research firm, you can either create your own unique survey with questions pertaining exclusively to your business or market area, or you may be able to pose a handful of questions as part of a larger survey being administered for a number of clients.

Some years ago, it was commonly believed that the products or services that tested best with online surveys were Internet-related or appealed to a technology-conscious audience. Today, with virtually every type of individual represented in fair measure on the Internet, online surveys can be used to test for a broad cross section of products and services. Plus, unlike telephone surveys, Internet surveys may be completed at the convenience of the participant, which means the individuals surveyed may take more time with their answers. Also, with the pervasive distaste among consumers for intrusive telephone contact, Internet surveys may be much better received. Should you decide to explore using online surveys, you'll find a searchable database of research firms online at http://www.quirks.com.

If you want to get up close and personal with your target audience and have very little or no money to invest in research, informal roundtable groups are a great idea. That's how Addie Swartz, the creator of Beacon Street Girls, gained invaluable information for her company's books and products. Over a period of one year, she and her associates held 30 groups—although they didn't call them focus groups, they called them ice-cream parties and they were held in people's homes.

Each group was composed of 6 to 9 girls between the ages of 9 and 12. When the girls entered the party, they were given a questionnaire on "pretty paper" that asked them questions about who they were and what was important to them, such as books, movies, subjects in school, sports, and pastime activities, and if they had brothers and sisters. Then they would all sit in a circle and start talking about things that were generated by the form.

In early groups, the topics focused primarily on what girls worry about and what Swartz's group could write that would help them. Later, the groups were held to refine the character development and appearance of the Beacon Street Girls. "Girls are detail-oriented at this age, and we had to redraw Charlotte's glasses four times and we changed her hair," says Swartz of the input the groups provided.

Today, Swartz's company, B*tween Productions, continues to obtain invaluable feedback and insight from its target audience via its Web site and by mail for very little cost. Four hundred girls from 33 states and 5 countries make up the International Tween Advisory Board and eagerly write to them about what they think of the Beacon Street Girls.

Like Swartz, you can initiate a far-reaching research program that reduces your risk when entering a new niche or modifying a product and service, yet spend very little money in the process. The trick is to assemble the best groups (and be sure to have multiple groups to verify the feedback is on track), ask the right questions, and listen carefully to the answers.

10

REINVENT
TRADITIONAL TACTICS

If you think mainstream media are priced out of reach for small businesses, think again. Now that you know the niche markets you'll tackle and understand your audience's preferences, you're ready to make the most efficient use of important marketing vehicles. The key is to use these traditional media—TV, radio, and magazines—in smart, more cost-effective ways.

#42 BENEFIT FROM
NEWLY AFFORDABLE CABLE TV

The network television spot is now a lumbering old dinosaur, useful primarily for raising big-brand awareness across massive target market groups. Even major consumer advertisers whose products require little or no explanation are moving to other media (and newer uses of television) as they watch audience numbers erode. Increasingly, the big splash ads—multi-million-dollar Super

Bowl spots come to mind—exist to drive customers to other touch points, such as Web sites, where there's deeper content.

Cable programming, on the other hand, offers advertisers a nimbler approach as well as lower rates. It's interesting to note that most consumers multitask when using electronic media and may watch television, go online, read a magazine, or open their mail at the same time. Multitasking consumers remember an advertised message if they're engaged in the program, and consequently focusing on TV versus other distractions. With cable TV, advertisers can reach narrowly defined target audiences by placing spots within programming that specifically meets their needs. From do-it-yourself shows to Court TV, you can reach audiences who are engaged in programming that addresses their unique interests.

Small-business owners are jumping into cable television because it allows them to put their messages in the proper context. You can reach women ages 25 to 49, for instance, who are interested in cooking, gardening, or interior design—you name it, there's a program to suit everyone. Plus, with cable you can place local spots in specific geographic market areas by working with your area cable systems. According to the *Pittsburgh Post-Gazette,* for instance, local commercials account for as many as 70 percent of the ads that appear on that region's cable stations and for roughly half the stations' revenues. Often, cable TV advertising is available in zones, so that you can reach just part of a single metropolitan area or several cities—it's up to you.

One cable company that's reaching out to small-business owners in markets from Los Angeles to Miami is Comcast, through its advertising sales division called Comcast Spotlight. In south Florida, for example, there are 19 different zones. You can advertise in a five- to ten-mile radius of your location or add zones. If you tell Comcast who your target audience is, your rep will use research from Nielsen Media Research, Scarborough, and others to help you choose between 40 to 60 different networks and the best-targeted programming. Ideally, you can create a spot package that includes some fixed position spots (within the shows you choose) and others that are rotated within a specific daypart on the networks you specify. For best results, Comcast recommends advertisers commit at least $1,500 a month to cable to achieve sufficient reach and frequency. That's less than half the cost of one newspaper ad in most major cities.

TV spots make your store, restaurant, product, or service "come alive" and reach a wide, yet qualified audience in a way that no other form of advertising can. But until recently, creative production was a major hurdle for local advertisers. It was just plain tough to compete with the big-budget spots from Pepsi and Burger King that cost hundreds of thousands of dollars to produce, that ran right along with local spots on cable TV. Now, however, the major cable systems are affiliating with production groups that produce spots of sufficient quality—though they probably aren't going to win any major awards—to stand up to those of big advertisers with deep pockets. For example, Comcast Spotlight, through a partnership with an outside production company, can produce a commercial for under $500 to about $1,200 (depending on the market), from scripting through shooting and postproduction, including a professional voice-over. Spots with actors and custom jingles cost more. Whether you own an ice-cream parlor, hardware store, or chiropractic office, if you work with your cable rep and the right production company, the quality of your locally produced cable TV spots should be entirely sufficient to convey your message and capture the attention of viewers.

Jim Anderson of Wizard of Claws is about to go into production on a new cable TV spot that he says will put more emphasis on his company's celebrity customers than the old one did. The Pembroke Pines, Florida, business owned by Jim's wife, Gilda Anderson, was founded in 2002 and places 2,500 puppies a year with owners such as Jennifer Love Hewitt, Eddie Jones of the Miami Heat, and the Ozzy Osborne family. Though just a few years old, this now-multimillion-dollar business derives revenue from its puppy boutique as well as sales of $10,000 Maltese and Yorkie puppies, among others. The Web site alone receives 7,000 to 10,000 unique visitors every day. Puppies are shown by appointment in what Anderson describes as a living room setting. Customers meet with a salesperson and view pictures of the breed, then individual puppies are brought in from the kennel. There are 21 employees, including 8 salespeople and 13 staff members, who care for the puppies.

Wizard of Claws began advertising on cable in September of 2004 and runs a combination of spots in rotation on networks including Animal Planet, Lifetime, Court TV (to reach women), ABC Family, and on some Nickelodeon programming that reaches parents watching with kids. It also runs fixed-position spots on Animal Planet from 7 to 8 PM and during Lifetime's Monday night movie. The spots air geographically in six zones surrounding the company's Pembroke Pines location. But Wizard of Claws also extends its buy to all of south Florida during special events, such as the Westminster Kennel Club dog show and the Eukanuba Night of Champions. Anderson says he prefers quality versus quantity and would rather air a $9 well-targeted spot than a $5 spot at midnight.

Anderson is surely doing something right, since sales immediately went up 30 percent to 40 percent in the first month Wizard of Claws began advertising on cable TV. Few things are more compelling than watching puppies on screen—making the company's "product" ideally suited to visual electronic media. Now, as the Wizard of Claws grows, it can afford to invest $10,000 a month in TV along with a mix of billboards, newspaper ads, online marketing, and special events, such as a joint promotion with Nickelodeon's Dora the Explorer during which the company gave away five dogs to families in need.

Cable works well, too, for small businesses on considerably leaner budgets. Richard Tallmadge runs what's by all accounts a highly successful cable TV campaign for $1,000 a month, plus occasional production costs that run in the hundreds of dollars, not thousands. He's the co-owner with his wife Cathy of The Restaurant Store in Key West, Florida. Not your typical retail outlet, it was founded in 1981 as a restaurant-equipment-and-supply business by a local Keys restaurateur. Tallmadge was in sales with one of the store's vendors before he and his wife bought the business in 1989 and eventually transformed it to include a retail store as well as a wholesale operation. Today, the business remains 70 percent wholesale with a two-person sales force servicing many of the hotels, restaurants, and bars in the Keys, and earns the remaining 30 percent of revenues from retail sales.

Unlike other restaurant-supply companies, the Tallmadges' retail space is filled with upscale products shown off by attractive lighting and fixtures. In 2003, the growing company bought a bakery that makes artisan bread, called Cole's Peace Artisan Bakery, and just recently moved it into their freestanding building right next to The Restaurant Store. Together, the two stores make an attractive destination for locals and the many tourists who visit this popular vacation area.

Tallmadge, an early adopter of cable TV advertising, has been using it successfully for approximately eight years to promote the retail side of the business. The Restaurant Store advertises on eight cable channels using Comcast in the Lower Keys, including the Food Channel (for obvious reasons), Lifetime (which Tallmadge says reaches housewives), and CNN and MSNBC to reach upscale consumers. His spots were a hit right from the start. In the company's first cable TV spot, the Tallmadges' small children, then ages two and three, were dressed in chef's outfits and placed in large stockpots in order to deliver their one line, "The Restaurant Store." The commercial was so popular that the children have been featured in all the store's spots throughout the years, including one that shows them marching by Key West landmarks set to the music of John Philip Sousa with the tag, "March on by to The Restaurant Store." Tourists and locals all enjoy—and remember—the spots. Says Tallmadge, "People come into the store and say . . . 'I love your commercials.'"

Each year, The Restaurant Store's TV schedule begins in mid-November, targeting locals who shop for holiday gifts, and continues through the Keys tourist season, which concludes at the end of April.

Although the spots run for six months out of the year, Tallmadge prefers monthly billing to keep the expenditure consistent. He works with Comcast Spotlight to assemble a targeted media buy, constructed largely of spots in rotation instead of fixed position, which Tallmadge feels are too costly. He budgets between 2½ percent and 3 percent of his company's $2.7 million in sales for carefully chosen marketing tactics. "What I love about cable is that it's like taking a dart and hitting exactly who you want," he says.

On the heels of the acquisition of Cole's Peace Artisan Bakery, Tallmadge has just created a unique cable TV campaign for the bakery that will rely on four to six different scenarios and run for the next three or four years. It's built around a new character, "Bread Man," who is a humorous take on a comic book superhero. If past experience is any indicator, tourists and neighbors alike will enjoy and remember Tallmadge's fun, local spots.

#43 MAXIMIZE RESPONSE WITH RADIO SPONSORSHIPS

For Tallmadge, like most successful advertisers, cable TV works synergistically with other media, including radio. Every year, from Thanksgiving through New Year's, The Restaurant Store airs a schedule of 30-second spots on popular Key West radio station 104.1, U.S. 1 Radio. Running five or six spots per day, according to Tallmadge, at $11 per spot, the radio campaign is an affordable complement to his more comprehensive TV schedule. This is a terrific example of a traditional use of radio advertising. And although this type of schedule might be cost-prohibitive for very small businesses in larger markets where the cost per spot is $250 or more, if you're in a small market where media costs are low, like Tallmadge is, chances are you can run a traditional spot schedule that yields high returns for your business.

Over the course of a week, radio reaches more than 228 million people—that's 94 percent of everyone age 12 and older in the

United States—according to Arbitron.[1] Radio doesn't discriminate. It reaches every ethnic group and economic level as well as America's affluent. Ninety-five percent of college grads as well as people age 18 and older in households with annual incomes of $75,000 or more listen to radio. Radio goes where we do. In fact, more than 80 percent of adults listen to radio while in their cars, and one-quarter of the population also listens at work. With formats from country to classical to suit every age and taste, radio can be used successfully to reach any demographic group.

There's a lot that's new in radio these days:

- Clutter is being reduced with initiatives such as "Less Is More" from Clear Channel and spot load-restriction policies from other radio groups. Studies show that listeners prefer more frequent and shorter breaks, and an increase in spot effectiveness results for advertisers. With shorter breaks, a higher percentage of the audience stays tuned through the second and third spots.
- In a study by Burke, Inc., an international research and consulting firm, a significant number of 30- and 15-second spots were shown to have recall scores equal to or greater than many 60-second commercials.[2] This proves that great spots, no matter what their length, generate strong recall, so advertisers need not always incur the cost of 60-second spots.
- An explosion in new radio formats, including Progressive Talk, JACK, CHILL, HURBAN, and others, attracts listeners who identify with the style of music that most closely reflects their tastes and personalities.
- Simulcast streaming on the Internet allows listeners to tune into their favorite radio stations while at their computers at work.

Add to these attributes radio's proven worth as a branding tool, and you have a good case for making local radio a part of your marketing mix.

Four Steps to Buying Time

Here's a quick, four-step primer on how to buy radio time:

Step 1. Focus on a narrow demographic. Prepare to make your media buy by reviewing the target audience profile you've already created (refer to Chapter 3). It should identify a narrow demographic target group and list any of their important characteristics or habits. Avoid the temptation to go after a broad audience. Remember, the more narrowly you focus your media buy, the less time and money you'll waste on unqualified leads and prospects. An example of a succinct target audience profile is: women, ages 25 to 54, who are employed outside the home, are homeowners, and reside in XYZ geographic market area.

Step 2. Contact the stations. A radio station's listenership is often predetermined based on its format. You may be surprised, however, by just who is listening to what—so be sure to contact numerous stations with a variety of formats and request their media kits. These kits are the basic selling tools used by radio stations and should include information on their audiences and programming. Speak to the individual station reps about your specific target audience, marketing budget, and needs, and request proposals that include ratings breakdowns for your target group.

Step 3. Evaluate the proposals. Look for three elements when evaluating each station's proposal: reach, frequency, and cost-per-point (CPP). "Reach" represents the number of individuals in your target audience group that will hear your marketing message. "Frequency" is the number of times those individuals will actually hear your message, not the number of times you run your spot. In other words, you'll need to run your spot with sufficient frequency for the members of your target audience to hear and remember your message.

The "cost-per-point" is what it will cost to reach 1 percent of your target audience population. All professional media buyers use CPP as the basis for their evaluation of cost-effectiveness, not the number of spots. You see, the bulk of your spots should run in dayparts that draw the largest percentage of your prospects, perhaps morning or afternoon drive time. A spot schedule that includes a lot of run-of-station (ROS) may deliver primarily low-cost spots that air in the middle of the night or during other dayparts when fewer of your targeted prospects are listening. So beware of any station that pushes the number of spots versus the quality of the spots you'll be buying, or offers you an extremely low-cost schedule that includes all ROS.

Step 4. Negotiate your buys. Once you have identified the stations and programming that will deliver your audience most cost-efficiently, it's time to negotiate a final media buy. It's often preferable to settle on a small number of core stations, rather than spread your dollars across many. In other words, first be certain that the advertising schedules on the core radio stations or programs you select will achieve the necessary frequency with your target audience for your message to penetrate. Then, as your company grows, you can add stations and programming to reach additional prospects.

But suppose you're in a major market where the CPP is sky-high, or you have a very limited budget and just want to get the most for your radio dollars. You still have some excellent options. Your best bet is to pick one radio station and get involved through sponsorships or partnerships. If you have a sufficient budget for a limited spot schedule and want to get the most bang for your buck, consider sponsoring a news, weather, or traffic report that airs at a fixed time each day. Although your reach may be somewhat limited, this will ensure that the same audience hears your message day after day so that you will achieve sufficient frequency. Also, along with your sponsorship, you'll often receive a five- to ten-second "billboard" to say something about your company, and you can negotiate to receive the first spot in the following commercial break. This is beneficial because spots that air first during a break tend to be heard by more of the audience.

Another option is to sponsor a program that links your product or service to a special interest. Remember 104.1, US-1 Radio in the Florida Keys? The station offers a program called "This Week in Fishing" that attracts every kind of related advertiser, from bait-and-tackle shops to seafood restaurants. Though the show airs weekly, ongoing promotions feature the name of the program's primary sponsor. This gives the advertiser continuous exposure to the station's entire listenership as well as in-program spots that reach listeners with a special interest in what they market.

Radio stations are promotional engines. An affordable way to get lots of on-air time is to sponsor one of their special events or an ongoing series of special promotions. It was just this type of radio involvement that helped put HoustonConnect.com on the map. Because his company is striving to be more than just a local dating service, Shmuel Gordon says, "We promote a lot of the community aspects of being single." Local area singles meet "to enjoy being single" on HoustonConnect.com and have formed their own groups, including a women's sushi group, another for mountain biking, and a number of single-parent groups.

Sponsoring singles parties was the perfect way for the young company to earn considerable, impactful airtime. For two years, HoustonConnect.com sponsored station events offered by 104.1 KRBE. Their morning-show DJ, Sam Malone, hosted Sammy's Singles Parties, and for a fixed cost per party, HoustonConnect.com received radio spots, ongoing mentions, and—best of all—was the subject of the DJ's morning show chatter. The morning after a party, members of HoustonConnect.com—who have their pictures posted on the dating Web site—would call the show to talk to Sammy and say what a great time they had. The DJ would make reference to the callers' profiles on HoustonConnect.com, and listeners would flock to the Web site to see the pictures of the callers who went to the singles parties. As you can imagine, this type of sponsorship was extremely effective in building memberships for the growing online company.

Gordon has also run other unique tie-ins in conjunction with station singles parties. Members of HoustonConnect.com post viewable profiles, and in one promotion that ran Monday through Friday for two weeks, Houstonians were invited to vote for their favorite profiles. Each week, one female and one male winner received a gift, such as a free dinner and a limo ride. To build votes and receive maximum attention for the promotion, DJs reminded listeners to "make sure you go to the profile of the week to vote for your favorite." These events have been so successful for HoustonConnect.com that it's expanded to sponsorships on other stations and has had a party cruise with 106.9, the Point.

Whether through special promotions or spots, radio success is all about entertaining the audience. For great examples of excellent on-air creative, you can listen to the winners of the coveted Mercury Awards at http://radiomercuryawards.com. While you'll hear überbudget spots from Molson, eBay, TBS, and Motel 6, you'll find that superior creativity doesn't just rest in the hands of the big advertisers. The 2005 winner in the 30-second category was a local market spot for Alert One Pest Control, created by Jason T. Skaggs of Zimmer Radio Group in Joplin, Missouri. Entitled "Ants," the very funny spot uses two voices. In a rapid-fire delivery, a humorous "ant-like" voice says the word *ant* and the second voice adds more syllables—*ant-Arctica, ant-ticipation, ant-Jemima,* and so on—until it becomes almost annoying. Then the copy continues, "Think that's irritating, try 'ants' all over your kitchen, in your garage, backyard, even your food . . . if you see one 'ant,' there are probably 8,541 more." The call to action follows, including phone numbers and information on where to see the company's ad.

Radio spot production is never a do-it-yourself job. But you need to understand a few basics to work effectively with your local production company or station.

A Good Radio Spot . . .

Holds the listener's attention. Comedy is most often used to grab and hold listeners. Most successful spots use humor to some degree, or at least put a very positive spin on the subject matter. You can also use sound, such as compelling music (a terrific jingle), or an unusual voice (the way Alert One Pest Control did in "Ants").

Relates the listener to the product or brand. Have you ever noticed that your favorite radio spots tell stories or present situations you can really relate to? A good spot presents some underlying truth that helps the listener connect to what's being marketed.

Is part of a campaign. It's human nature to be on the lookout for something "new." In fact, scientists tell us that our brains alert to new information. If you create a campaign, listeners will associate each new ad with previous ones and listen for the latest twist. This actually helps to extend your message more successfully than if you run unrelated spots.

Has great on-air talent. You don't need a large cast, but you do need a well-qualified one. This is not the time to hire your brother-in-law who wants to be in show business. Wonderful, professional voice-over talent is available nationwide, and you should be sure to pick the right voices for your spots.

Includes a payoff. This can be the resolution of the humorous situation or some final bit of information that helps listeners take advantage of what you offer. If your call to action includes a telephone number or a URL, make it easy to remember and tie it in with your company name or message.

#44 LEARN SMART WAYS
TO USE MAGAZINES

Like the diversity in cable TV programming and radio station formats, there is quite literally a magazine to fit the needs of every target audience. As you've seen throughout this book, marketing success involves reaching prospects through synergistic media. And, as a 2004 CrossMedia study by Dynamic Logic revealed, magazine advertising can actually outperform other media—including television and Internet ads—in generating "purchase intent" when tossed into your media mix.[3] Magazines can increase your advertising ROI when they're part of a multimedia marketing program. In the CrossMedia study, magazines' incremental effect was shown to be nearly twice as powerful as that of television and the Internet combined when it came to influencing purchase behavior.

Think about how other media advertising, including television and the Internet, requires brief top-level messages (with perhaps the exception of longer-format direct-response TV spots and infomercials). Magazine ads, on the other hand, let you tell an in-depth story, particularly if you use full-page and other large ad units, and allow you to provide all the information your prospects need to make a buying decision. If you have a new product or service and want to educate your prospects, or if you're introducing new features of an existing product or service, this ability to convey deeper information can be particularly beneficial. Best of all, the variety of advertising options offered by the enormous range of trade and consumer magazines makes it easy and affordable to include magazines in your marketing mix.

To create a low-waste, high-return magazine advertising program, it's essential to start with a comprehensive understanding of your customers and how they learn about, and use, what you market. Take, for example, the makers of Sea Eagle inflatable boats and kayaks. You'll probably remember this successful family-owned business, Harrison-Hoge Industries, Inc., from Chapter 3. Because the company's kayaks are inflatable, and not designed specifically for performance or speed, their buyers aren't necessarily kayaking enthusiasts. In fact, the company's targeted prospects—80 percent of whom are male, 35 to 70 years old, often retired professionals, with incomes of $100,000 plus—are more likely to buy inflatable boats to use along with their motor homes or yachts.

This family business, run for the past decade by President Cecil Hoge, Jr., with the help of his brother, Vice President John Hoge, has a long history of successful sales going back to the early 1950s, when it sold fishing lures, and the 1960s when the company began selling boats. Their father, Cecil Hoge, Sr., wrote four marketing books, but the company's (now in-house) advertising agency goes back even farther to when their grandfather began it in 1919.

Last year, Harrison-Hoge Industries enjoyed nearly $8 million in annual sales, and magazine advertising is a strong part of the company's multimedia strategy. From January through June, a core group of 20 publications carry ads in sizes ranging from one-sixth of a page to a full page, with one-third-page ads being the predominant unit.

Based on the target audience demographics and what the Hoges know about how their customers use their products, the magazine schedule includes primarily general-interest publications with strong male readerships that meet the company's age and affluence requirements, as well as some vertical publications targeted by special interest. Here's a short list of some of the publications the company uses:

- *Popular Science*
- *Field and Stream*
- *Outdoor Life*
- *Highways*
- *National Geographic*
- *Outside*
- *U.S. News & World Report*
- *Newsweek*

- *Trailer Life*
- *Canoe and Kayak*
- *New York Times Magazine*
- *Paddler*
- AARP publications

All ads are keycoded and tracked, although, as Cecil Hoge notes, "We could be reaching someone many different ways." The company receives 150 to 200 requests every day for its print catalog, and the Web site (SeaEagle.com) receives a million visitors per year. Not bad for a small business with a staff of 34!

Tips for Including Magazines in Your Media Mix

Ready to make magazines part of your media mix? Here are seven helpful tips:

1. **Use direct-response sections.** Many national magazines have sections designed just to accommodate smaller advertisers. These sections, typically located in the back of the publication, work best for direct-response ads that offer products or catalogs. Here you'll see many fractional page ads, such as one-third-page or one-sixth-page ads, like the ones favored by Harrison-Hoge Industries. These direct-response advertising sections tend to draw solid readerships scores because subscribers habitually peruse them looking for a wide range of products.

2. **Look for regional editions.** Though at first glance the national magazine of your choice may appear to be priced out of reach, don't give up. A select number of national magazines offer regional advertising opportunities at more affordable rates. Regional ads are often sold in full-page increments only, making them indistinguishable from the national ads in the rest of the magazine. So for the cost of a regional buy, your full-page ad can

have the same impact on readers as those from Nike or Revlon, and you'll pay significantly less.

3. Use vertical publications. If you're a b2b (business-to-business) marketer, you may find advertising in vertical publications considerably more affordable than the "horizontal" business press with gigantic circulations, such as the major newsweeklies. Depending on your target audience, you'll find special-interest publications in every arena. If you're marketing presentation technology, there's *Presentations* magazine. Want to market your product as a corporate employee incentive? There's *Incentive* magazine. There are also publications that target individuals by title, such as *CMO* magazine, which is read by chief marketing officers in a variety of industries.

4. Investigate combo buys. You may remember from Chapter 3 that many media offer special rates when you buy several of their properties. For example, some magazines offer print advertising, online advertising, e-newsletters, and card decks to reach their subscribers. So you can cost-efficiently increase your frequency with a magazine's subscriber base by negotiating combo buys that include multiple media properties, such as ads in a print magazine and on its Web site.

5. Obtain subscriber lists. In Chapter 5, I told you how Mark Sussman, president of Dance Distributors, advertised in *Dance Teacher Magazine* and used the publication's subscriber list to mail posters to dance studios. Some magazines offer their mailing lists as a bonus to advertisers at no additional cost, or you can rent them. This allows you to take advantage of direct mail in combination with your print advertising to reach the same subscriber base, or simply a portion of it. So you can affordably increase your frequency and make a more in-depth pitch via direct mail to a highly qualified audience.

6. Use local, specialty magazines. Glossy magazines abound in major markets nationwide. Many of them cater to specific areas of interest and readership groups. You'll remember that Farrey's Lighting and Bath uses *Selecta* to reach upscale Latinos in the Miami area, for example. Decorating, real estate, and parenting magazines, for example, are available in many markets. These publications often work best when used in combination with other local media.

7. Track all responses. Never place a single, solitary ad unless it's keycoded. This is the only way to track what works and what doesn't. Coding is simple, just include a special letter and/or number in your response mechanism so that you can identify all leads and traffic each ad generates. Of course, just as Cecil Hoge mentioned, there will be great overlap if your media campaign is effectively reaching a core of qualified prospects. Some prospects will tell you they responded to your ad on the Web, when your magazine ads were actually responsible for increasing their awareness of your company and predisposing them to respond to your online advertising. Nonetheless, the tracking data you obtain will still be quite useful in helping you fine-tune your media buy.

Cable TV, radio, and magazines allow you to select just the right venues to reach your target audience in the best context. With careful shopping and negotiation, you can put together a low-cost campaign that includes these important media in your marketing mix.

11

TRY SOMETHING NEW

Throughout this book, you've learned smart, affordable ways to use a full range of proven marketing tactics, from e-newsletters to cable TV and radio. In this chapter, I'll share my final three ways to produce superior results on a limited budget. It's a triumvirate of marketing tactics that may be quite new to you. So as they used to say on the wonderfully original, classic British TV series, *Monty Python's Flying Circus,* "And now for something completely different."

#45 REACH BIG-SCREEN AUDIENCES

Can you guess which is the fastest-growing major advertising medium after the Internet? It's cinema advertising that's catching the attention of large and small advertisers alike. Big-budget marketers, including Coca-Cola, Adidas, and Procter & Gamble, are moving some of their money out of network television and putting it into what are called "rolling stock" ads, or sound and motion cinema spots, while the bulk of small-business advertisers are using still-image advertising.

Almost one-third of the U.S. population goes to the movies every month, and these moviegoers are fairly young and affluent, according to a 2004 "Nielsen Cinema Audience Report."[1] Nearly 20 percent are in the 18-year-old to 24-year-old age group, and about 40 percent fall between the ages of 25 and 54. And don't believe what you may have heard about the audience composition. Studies show that 52 percent of moviegoers are male and 48 percent are female. So, it's pretty evenly split between adult men and women. In 2004, 35 percent of all moviegoers were college graduates or more highly educated, and the median household income among moviegoers was $66,000. In all, this makes moviegoers a desirable audience for many types of small businesses.

The big advantage of cinema advertising is its impact on the audience. Adults who frequent the theater arrive an average of 19 minutes early and are exposed to an array of marketing media, including video programming in the lobby, posters, coupons and counter cards, and even advertising on popcorn bags. Cinema ads reach an engaged, "captive" audience of viewers. They're not multitasking when exposed to cinema advertising—such as watching television while going online—and this pays off in advertising effectiveness. A 2004 study conducted by TNS and sponsored by Screenvision found that moviegoers who saw in-theater ads were 44 percent more likely to remember them than consumers who saw ads on television.[2] This survey, which included 2,000 moviegoers in 5 cities, also discovered that they were 70 percent more likely to correctly identify the advertised brands in cinema ads than in TV commercials.

Another significant advantage of cinema advertising is the flexibility it allows small-business owners to geographically target a quality audience. More than 27,000 of the total 37,000 movie screens in the United States run advertising, so it's likely that you can place your ads in a multiplex near you.

The two predominant sales units for cinema advertising are Screenvision and National CineMedia. Screenvision represents the largest national network in the United States, with nearly 15,000 screens, including those at Loews Cineplex, Carmike Cinemas, Cinemark, and Pacific theaters. Its business unit, Screenvision Direct, has about 150 sales reps that work with small businesses nationwide and an in-house creative department that produces cinema advertising slides for local advertisers. You're probably familiar with these slides that are screened during a preshow (not after the announced movie time) that consist of trivia and pop-up quizzes from popular movies, advertising, and the theater's own content. National CineMedia is the advertising and marketing sales division of Regal Entertainment Group and AMC Entertainment, the nation's two largest movie theater owners, though at this writing a planned merger between Loews Cineplex and AMC could cause a reshuffling of those group's advertising sales forces.

Cinema advertising costs are surprisingly low. You can supply photos to be made into cinema slides at little or no additional cost, and some theater chains offer to connect local business owners with their production partners to produce affordable sound and motion spots. Although the media rates will vary depending on the theater and location, they're generally based on a weekly rate per screen. Advertisers must buy all screens in the theaters they choose. For example, if your local theater has 10 screens, you might pay as little as $25 weekly per screen, for a total of $1,000 per month, and reach all moviegoers who see every movie in that theater. Because the average moviegoer may see one movie a month, it's a good idea to buy a long-term schedule to keep top-of-mind and build recognition.

To give you a good idea of what can be accomplished with cinema advertising, let's look at two very different types of small businesses—both targeting women.

Gymkhana Gymnastics of Pittsburgh, Pennsylvania, has specialized in gymnastic classes for children since 1978. Business partners Elliott Sanft and Ed Swerdlow were both on the gymnastic team at the University of Pittsburgh. Sanft, an economics major, was one year ahead of Swerdlow, who majored in physical education, and after graduation they combined Sanft's business background with Swerdlow's teaching training to create Gymkhana. "Originally, we both taught and coached and did the janitorial work and the paperwork and everything else," says Sanft. Today, the partners have 3,500 students in three expansive facilities, including a 14,000-square-foot ice rink they bought and transformed.

The partners have identified women with children, from newborns up to 12 years of age, as their primary target audience, and their largest enrollment is in the 2½- to 6-year-old age group. "When we started our business, we were marketing gymnastics classes for children and it was growing, but a tough sell," says Sanft. It wasn't until Gymkhana began marketing the benefits its classes provided—balance, coordination, self-confidence—that the marketing began to achieve higher levels of success. According to Sanft, "Students can sign up for our program without any interest in gymnastics and there are benefits that apply to baseball, football, cheerleading programs, and anything else the children will participate in . . . we use gymnastics to get there."

Gymkhana Gymnastics primarily relies on cinema advertising to improve name awareness as part of a campaign that includes direct mail, a short television schedule, and advertising in a local parenting publication, *Pittsburgh Parent.* Affordability is important to Sanft, and cinema advertising certainly fits the bill. The company's still-image ads run in 2 well-located multiplexes on a total of 11 screens, 3 slides per screen. Their cost is just $116 per screen per month, or $1,276. There's no costly production, and Gymkhana has been running the same ad successfully for two years. It also benefits from promotions courtesy of Screenvision Direct and Loews. As an advertiser, they've received a countertop display that's a replica of their on-screen ad plus giveaways to display along with it, including free passes and invitations to free preview showings for children.

Sanft even credits his cinema advertising with helping to effectively build awareness that translates to coverage in local news.

"In an Olympic year, all the local news stations and publications are looking for related stories to gymnastics, so since we're the first thing that comes to their minds, they give us a call."

Women's Integrated Healthcare of Grapevine, Texas, has also used cinema advertising as a branding tool. Although you might not think of this group medical practice as a small business, one of its founding partners, Dr. Barbara Coulter-Smith, stresses that like any other business today it must win and keep clients.

Founded in 2001 in an area between Dallas and Fort Worth, the four-physician group differentiates itself by being an all-female ob-gyn practice. Early on, the doctors knew they needed a creative way to bring in new clients. They had begun advertising in newspapers and local magazines when they were contacted by Screenvision Direct. According to Coulter-Smith, "Advertising is new for physicians, so two of us said, no way, and two others said, why not?" In 2003, they decided to jump in, using 10 screens at one theater on a budget of $1,600 per month. The partners were quickly convinced they'd made the right move. They were so happy with the results that in 2004, Coulter-Smith says they increased their cinema advertising buy to a total of 37 screens in 2 theaters, and now consider the budget of $4,000 per month well spent. Advertising results are tracked and cinema advertising is always among the top two most popular sources of new patients, along with the *Fort Worth Star Telegram*.

For Women's Integrated Healthcare, cinema advertising attracts a somewhat different client base than do newspaper ads. "Households turn over here about every 22 months," says Coulter-Smith. The cinema advertising attracts younger, more transient, and affluent stay-at-home moms, while the clients who are generated from newspaper advertising tend to be professionals and working people.

Like Gymkhana, Women's Integrated Healthcare successfully uses still-image advertising. Its slide features a photograph of the partners (all dressed in lavender, not white lab coats). The copy communicates that theirs is an all-female ob-gyn practice offering limited evening and weekend hours, and includes the company name and an easy-to-remember phone number, 416-BABY. "It's branded us," says Coulter-Smith, whose successful practice has projected gross billings of $7 million in 2005 and is about to expand to include another physician.

#46 GET CLOSE TO CUSTOMERS WITH EXPERIENTIAL MARKETING

Which would have a bigger impact on your intention to buy a particular product—reading about it in an ad or trying it out first-hand? The fact is, real-life experiences shape our opinions and buying preferences more profoundly than what we see in advertising or hear from our friends. That's the driving force behind the new wave of "experiential marketing," which uses events to bring customers into one-on-one contact with a product to create memorable experiences. It's the difference between telling people about the features and benefits of your product and allowing them to experience these benefits for themselves.

Major businesses use experiential marketing to great advantage. For example, Microsoft hired a leading experiential marketing firm to introduce business travelers to its Tablet PC by setting up staffed demonstration stations in highly trafficked airport terminals in major hubs across the United States and select office building lobbies in Chicago and New York City. But you don't have to create an extravagant demonstration space to be effective. Any number of venues will work for your small business, including malls, fairs, retail stores, and restaurants, just so long as they support the theme of your event and foster interaction.

In a 2005 Experiential Marketing Survey by Jack Morton Worldwide, 70 percent of consumers said that participating in a live marketing experience would increase their purchase consideration, and close to 60 percent said it would result in a quicker purchase.[3] The study also showed that the effect of experiential marketing is strongest among youth and female consumers. Nearly 80 percent of teens stated experiential marketing would increase purchase consideration, and 60 percent of women said it would be more likely to lead them to actually purchase a product than would TV or the Internet. It's also worth noting that more than 80 percent of Hispanic females indicated that participating in a live marketing event would make them more receptive to future advertising.

Experiential Marketing Offers Strong Advantages

It allows a small marketer to stand out in a highly competitive arena. For example, a small-business owner who invented a new toy was elated when he was finally able to convince a major chain to carry it. Unfortunately, the product languished on the shelves and it soon became clear that it was doomed to be overlooked in major retail stores where it was surrounded by thousands of other products with well-known brand names. So the inventor began taking booths at craft shows to allow children to play with the toy. Once parents and kids had an opportunity to really see and experience it, his invention was a hit. Soon he added more experiential marketing venues, including Girl Scout meetings and other kid-friendly events across the country.

It's a low-cost way to introduce a new product. Unlike major marketers that can spend millions launching new products, small-business owners who need to get the most bang for the buck can realize great results by putting their products in front of just the right people. A well-planned experiential marketing event can give your new product the liftoff it needs. The key to a successful experiential marketing event is to choose a venue that will attract the right crowd (such as a mall, fair, or even street marketing), or create your own event and invite your best prospects. Keep in mind that it's possible to have a successful event yet produce an unsuccessful marketing experience. Suppose you've created a new line of hair accessories. You could hold a party in a trendy hair salon, pack it with models sporting your new hair accessories along with 100 happy revelers. But if the attendees are the wrong age, gender, or economic group, you won't advance your marketing cause.

It's a great way to earn immediate sales. Ever hear of Tupperware parties? Proven popular since way back when, home parties give customers a chance to experience the benefits of a product they can't buy elsewhere. In fact, one handbag designer who launched her line almost exclusively through home parties hosted primarily by stay-at-home moms built a $10 million business in just a few short years. Many types of events that integrate entertainment with the opportunity to test a product are extremely well received. In the Jack Morton survey, 84 percent of women said they'd bring family or friends to a live marketing experience, and 75 percent said they'd tell others about the experience.[4] The event itself is what separates experiential marketing from traditional "sampling," and it's the fun and excitement of participating that entice customers to make purchases.

It makes a one-on-one connection between your customer and product. The cliché "seeing is believing" really rings true when it comes to experiential marketing. When the Jack Morton survey measured the effectiveness of experiential marketing in 14 product and service categories, in 11 out of 14, consumers said their preferred means of learning about new products and services was by experiencing them for themselves or hearing about them from someone they knew. By giving your prospects an opportunity to interact with your product in a memorable way, you create a strong emotional tie and lay the groundwork for a loyal customer relationship.

It allows for product demonstration. Suppose you have a product that's so new and different customers have to really see it in action. Experiential marketing allows you to demonstrate the product in a way that helps people become at ease with it—even if it involves new technology. Have you ever seen the small automatic vacuum cleaner, called Roomba, that can zip around the floor on its own? When its inventors at iRobot Corporation introduced it to focus groups, participants were reported to be skeptical until they saw the small machine in action. Guided by this input, the company's founders pursued sales through demonstration-friendly stores, including The Sharper Image and Brookstone, so even though the inventors themselves weren't present demonstrating the product, their prospective customers could nonetheless interact with the small vacuum as it moved about the floor.

It encourages customer trial. When it comes to successful experiential marketing, smaller events in intimate settings are generally preferred over large events with too many people. Not only do smaller events allow you to get close to your customers and maximize one-on-one interaction, they give everyone a chance to try out your product. Face-to-face dialogue and the ability to share the experience with others are among the top factors consumers say make an event most interesting to them. So avoid the crush and give all attendees a positive experience with your product. And because smaller events cost less, you'll save money, too.

It's guaranteed to build buzz. Experiential marketing has an extended impact by virtue of building word of mouth. Three quarters of the consumers surveyed by Jack Morton said they would be extremely or very likely to tell others after participating in a live marketing event. Furthermore, eight out of ten people who had actually participated in experiential marketing in the past said they had told others about their experience.

Anywhere you can effectively interact with customers can be an experiential marketing venue, whether at craft shows, home parties, invitation-only events in restaurants or nightclubs, staged sites in the local mall, or in an office building lobby. Busy street corners have often become the locus for guerrilla marketing events.

Of course, supermarkets are well-known venues for offering tasty samples to shoppers. But how do you transform ho-hum sampling into experiential marketing and turn a supermarket demonstration on its ear? Meet Paula White, CEO and cofounder with husband Chris, of 600 Lb. Gorillas, Inc., the Wrentham, Massachusetts, makers of prepared, frozen cookie dough. When the couple founded their company in 1999, they knew they'd be competing with Pillsbury and Nestlé and would need an extraordinary way to stand out. Instead of a commonplace name for their brand, such as White's Cookies, they decided to go with something bold and fun right from the start that would help them build buzz and capture the attention of the media. They dreamed up the name 600 Lb. Gorillas, built a hut with a thatched roof, and donned safari clothing to do their first food show, The Taste of Boston, where they handed out hot cookies and cold milk to consumers. Along with the free cookies, they also passed out survey cards for consumers to fill out that asked where they shopped.

Back then, the Whites didn't even have a real package design, let alone a presence in stores. So although local newspapers were interested in covering them, the press told Paula White to call when the cookies were actually available. White is a "big fan" as she says of cold calling and soon got in to see buyers at the local stores. Fortunately, she was armed with 2,000 cards from consumers who said they would buy the cookie product if it were in the stores. For every appointment Paula White booked, she and Chris (who created the recipe) went dressed in their safari costumes and brought along their postcards and plenty of cookies and milk. Smart marketer that she is, White also told the store buyers about the newspaper coverage just ready and waiting. According to White, "Once we got in one store, I went to its competitor and said we're going to have all this publicity and be available at your competition." Then, she says, "After we got in the two largest stores, the smaller stores followed." True to form, six months later when her product was in Boston-area stores, White went back to the media and received the promised stories in the *Boston Globe, Boston Herald,* and the *Boston Phoenix,* and even some local TV coverage.

Experiential marketing was the catapult that drove everything, from media attention, a positive reaction in sales calls, and eventually the product itself. Every Friday, Saturday, and Sunday for two years, the Whites donned their costumes and packed up their thatched hut to put on three-hour sampling events in higher-volume supermarkets, with the goal of selling 60 boxes each day. During the summers, they went to stores where people on vacation would be exposed to their product and remember the cookies when they went back to their stores at home. To add to the fun at their supermarket demonstrations, in 2002, White started having someone in a guerrilla costume attend most live events. "We're able to get people's attention long enough for them to try the product, and then they're sold," she says.

The quality of the product, which is all natural with no hydrogenated oils, certainly keeps customers coming back. In April of 2005, prepared cookie dough from 600 Lb. Gorillas was put through a taste test by *The Washington Post* and came out the number one winner, beating out competing products from Pillsbury and Nestlé among others. Today, cookie dough from 600 Lb. Gorillas is sold in about 600 supermarkets, 150 club stores, including BJ's Wholesale Clubs on the East Coast, and convenience stores. And with projected sales of $2.5 million in 2005, for the Whites, success is sweet.

#47 SEND MAT RELEASES
TO PAPERS NATIONWIDE

Here's a tactic you've probably never heard of, yet it's commonly used by Fortune 100 companies on a continuing basis. If you happen to be among the people who believe that all the stories that appear in the newspaper are created by newspeople who are writing copy for the single purpose of informing readers, then you may find this everyday publishing practice a bit surprising. You see, most newspapers are dramatically understaffed and editors are overworked. On a daily basis, most papers, with the exception of the biggest and richest, are short on staff and have editorial "holes" to fill. Consequently, major services provide "mat" releases, articles prewritten and ready for publication. Most of these articles are written by or for companies to meet their public relations goals, and they pay the services for distributing their articles in the form of mat releases to newspapers nationwide.

Newspaper editorial is generally perceived as more "credible" than the advertising carried by the same papers, so mat releases are an effective way to reach and persuade readers. For example, suppose you owned a financial planning company. For less than the cost of one decent-size ad in a single daily newspaper, you could create an article to be distributed with your byline (your name as author), such as "Four Tips for Planning a Safe Retirement." This article might get picked up by several thousand newspapers across the country and generate dozens of qualified leads or more.

There are three primary mat release services: Metro Editorial Services, NAPS (North American Precis Syndicate), and ARA, which distributes online only. Metro Editorial Services has been distributing mat releases since 1933 and has a pricing structure that easily fits the needs of small-business owners. Its monthly editorial packages are distributed in camera-ready hard copy and on CD-ROM to 7,000 daily and weekly newspapers throughout North America (including editors at the top 200 dailies) and are accessed online by 2,000 more. The average size of a feature is between 11 and 14 column inches, including a photo, and costs between $2,255 and $2,870. In addition to the monthly editorial packages, themed special editions, such as Easy Living and Back to School, reach editors as they're planning their own special sections.

When creating your company's mat release, you can either provide background information and have the service create the article for you or write it yourself. The most important thing to keep in mind is that, with the exception of articles written specifically to tie in with holidays such as Thanksgiving and Christmas, your story should be "evergreen," with a minimum shelf life of six months. That's because the editors who receive the copy may choose to use it at any time. This can add long-term value, since your piece may continue to get placed for many months in newspapers across the country. Some services guarantee a minimum of 25 placements and state that typical results may be as high as 400 placements per release. Because your article is sent in camera-ready form on CD-ROM or downloaded directly from the Internet, it's likely that it will run completely as you submit it, not heavily edited or rewritten as would be the case with a typical press release.

There's absolutely no reason this valuable marketing tactic should stay a relative secret. Now that you know how to get low-cost access to thousands of newspapers, it's only a matter of shaping your editorial message to spread the word about your small business.

12

PUT IT ALL TOGETHER

Are you feeling like a kid in a candy store yet? With so many different ideas and wonderful ways to grow your small business, choosing just the right group of tactics can be tricky.

Some business owners have a tendency to go overboard and try too many different kinds of marketing tactics—which can quickly lead to burnout, overwork, and wasted marketing dollars. With too many tactics, you can feel overwhelmed and lack the time it takes to properly manage your program and follow up with leads or customers.

On the flip side, small-business owners are notoriously risk-averse. A surprisingly high percentage who fear making the wrong choices do too little or nothing at all, and hesitate to allocate a percentage of sales dollars to marketing tactics. As a result, they watch their businesses stagnate or, worse yet, spiral slowly downward. Only when their businesses are truly failing do they finally take the leap into the smart marketing tactics they might have benefited from all along. Unfortunately, at this point it's often too late. As any of the successful small-business owners profiled in this book will tell you, marketing is a process that requires consistent effort over a period of time, and results are rarely achieved overnight.

Stephen Marder, whose new Internet business, Golden Oak Stables, is already doing $1 million in sales, is an entrepreneur who also happens to have a PhD in finance. He was founding director of the Pacific Islands Small Business Development Center in Micronesia, as well as the former director of the Center for Economic Development of the University of Minnesota at Duluth. Want to know what Marder allocates for his marketing budget? He recommends setting aside up to 20 percent of sales to marketing programs, and at present his company is spending approximately 15 percent. This is one small-business owner who practices what he preaches and clearly benefits by it.

The key to successfully assembling a marketing program is to budget sufficient funds and focus on a small group of affordable tactics that you can manage along with the day-to-day operation of your growing business.

#48 COMBINE SALES WITH MARKETING

Marketing exists to support sales. It can raise awareness, inform and educate, influence public opinion, and induce prospects to act. But marketing can't replace the human element that adds the heat to close sales. When you combine sales activities with a strong marketing campaign, you deliver an effective one-two punch. Even if you sell exclusively through an e-commerce site, customers want to know about the people and the company behind the site, and will often make their buying decisions based on the customer experience—how you deal with them one-on-one online or by telephone for customer service and sales.

As you create your marketing program, choose only as many tactics as you can schedule based on the projected time and effort it will take to handle the ensuing sales contacts. Remember Jeff

Porro of Porro & Associates from Chapter 6, who used dimensional mail to reach prospects? He sent only as many boxes per week as he could comfortably follow up by phone and e-mail. He also allowed time to handle the meetings that resulted from his campaign. Had he sent all 150 of his dimensional mailers at once, he would have been unable to properly handle the number of responses—wasting his investment and missing out on the opportunity to close new clients.

Answer Three Important Questions

To gauge just how much time you should safely allow for your sales activities, candidly answer the following questions:

1. **At what points in the sales cycle must your company make one-to-one contact with prospects?** Throughout this book, you've seen how important it is to touch prospects often through a combination of sales and marketing tactics. Marketing tools and tactics can be used specifically to open the door to sales contact. Advertising, for example, reaches new prospects and produces leads that may be followed up by phone calls. Later, you can add these prospects to your database and send e-mail or direct mail to provide a hook for another follow-up sales call. Once you've moved your prospects through the sales cycle with a combination of sales and marketing, it's bound to be one-to-one contact that adds the final heat to close.

2. **Who in your company will be responsible for sales?** If you're the chief cook and bottle washer, you may have very little time for sales activities. So it's smart to choose the marketing tactics in this book that lead to the least amount of face time with prospects. Otherwise you may fall into the trap of running marketing campaigns and then not following up. Lack of follow-up can give prospects a negative impression of your company, and marketing becomes a wasteful exercise when important contacts fall through the cracks.

This happens most in companies where the person primarily responsible for sales is working overtime to get the actual business work accomplished and has little time for anything else.

Small businesses with two or more people on staff can engage in more intensive sales activities. Just be sure the person designated as responsible for sales really wants to be in that position and excels at it.

If you have a sales staff, your mandate is to set up a marketing program designed to produce the maximum number of opportunities to interact one-on-one with customers. As you do your planning, keep in mind that your marketing campaign will be much more effective if you have buy-in from the sales staff. Hold regularly scheduled meetings and establish strong and open lines of communication between sales and marketing. Get input from sales concerning customers' needs and preferences and any inroads being made by your competition in order to help keep your marketing on track. And present your marketing strategies and tactics to the sales force to get their input prior to launching any marketing campaign.

3. What is your projected annual marketing budget? Many types of public relations as well as networking activities are extremely low in cost when it comes to out-of-pocket expenses, yet they're prodigiously time-intensive. As you set up your campaign, look realistically at your projected budget and assign marketing tactics you can comfortably afford to carry out with enough frequency to achieve success. Then, just fill in the gaps with sales activities that require little out-of-pocket expense. As your business grows and your marketing budget increases, you can always add additional, higher-ticket marketing tactics and reduce your reliance on sales activities.

#49 CHOOSE THE RIGHT TACTICS

When developing your own marketing program, take your cue from the more than 30 success stories featured in this book.

All the small-business owners profiled are actively marketing using media mixes composed of a short list of core tactics. Even the small businesses with larger marketing budgets, such as Dance Distributors and Harrison-Hoge Industries, have committed to just a handful of the right marketing tactics and use them with enough frequency to powerfully impact sales.

The question is, How do you find the right marketing mix? The best way is to match your tactics to the changing needs of your prospects as they move through the sales cycle. At any given time, you'll have cold prospects who know little or nothing about you, warm prospects who are currently being exposed to your campaign, and hot prospects who are nearly ready to close. My formula for a great media mix is to have at least one sales and one marketing tactic for each of these three stages.

Motivate Cold, Warm, and Hot Prospects

Here's a list of tactics that effectively reach and motivate prospects as they enter and pass through your sales cycle. Following each tactic you'll see the name of the small business profiled in this book for its success with that tactic.

Marketing tactics for cold prospects:

- **Online paid search.** Color Creek Fiber Art, Sea Eagle (Harrison-Hoge Industries), plan3D, Inc., the Healthy Holistic Pet, Golden Oak Stables
- **Online advertising.** Sea Eagle (Harrison-Hoge Industries), plan3D, Inc.
- **Print advertising.** Farrey's Lighting and Bath, Sea Eagle (Harrison-Hoge Industries), Women's Integrated Healthcare, Alianza Mortgage
- **Cable TV.** The Restaurant Store, Wizard of Claws

- **Public relations.** Fran's Chocolates, Modern Bin, 600 Lb. Gorillas, e.l.f. Cosmetics, Willow, Stanley's Tavern, Nite Lites, Beacon Street Girls (B*tween Productions)
- **Experiential marketing.** 600 Lb. Gorillas, O'Keeffe's Company
- **Dimensional mail.** Porro & Associates
- **Marriage mail.** Lafayette Tire and Auto
- **Events.** Nite Lites, Alianza Mortgage, Quadrille Quilting, Changing Course, Willow, HoustonConnect.com
- **Radio.** HoustonConnect.com, The Restaurant Store
- **Out-of-home.** Willow, HoustonConnect.com
- **Cinema.** Gymkhana, Women's Integrated Healthcare
- **Place-based.** Dance Distributors, Nite Lites

Sales tactics for cold prospects:

- **Cold calls.** 600 Lb. Gorillas
- **Networking.** Sanders Financial Management, Inc.

Marketing tactics for warm prospects:

- **E-mail to opt-in lists.** Dance Distributors, Porro & Associates, ShopCloseBuy.com, Media Specialists, Inc., *DailyCandy*
- **Customer rewards program.** Stanley's Tavern, Bike Friday, Golden Oak Stables
- **Customer events.** Two Sisters Catering, Stanley's Tavern, HoustonConnect.com
- **Web sites dedicated to community.** Bike Friday, Beacon Street Girls (B*tween Productions), ShopCloseBuy.com, Aurora Pages Press
- **Direct mail to in-house lists.** Porro & Associates, Quadrille Quilting
- Most forms of **Advertising** (with the exception of paid search, classified, and directory ads) and **PR** are primary tactics for reaching warm as well as cold prospects.

Sales tactics for warm prospects:

- **Follow-up calls, meetings, and presentations.** 600 Lb. Gorillas, O'Keeffe's Company, e.l.f. Cosmetics
- **Follow-up sales letters.**
- **Networking.** Sanders Financial Management, Inc.

Marketing and sales tactics for hot prospects. These prospects have been systematically exposed to all the cold and warm sales and marketing tactics as they moved through your sales cycle. Depending on your type of business and what you market, hot prospects may respond to marketing tactics such as direct-mail or e-mail solicitations that include special incentives. Plus, for many small-business owners, closing requires one-on-one sales, whether to present a proposal or make a presentation.

#50 CREATE YOUR OWN MARKETING PROGRAM

In the introduction to this book, you learned the importance of looking at your competition and building your marketing themes around a competitive advantage.

Steps for Conducting a Competitive Analysis

The first step in achieving that goal—and in creating an effective marketing plan—is to conduct a simple competitive analysis. It's fast, easy, and free. Just follow these important steps:

Make a comprehensive list of competitors. Where might your prospective customers go to buy what you sell? Any company that your customers or clients may turn to for a product or service like yours should be viewed as a competitor, including superstores or even megasites on the Web. You may feel that you compete solely with other small businesses that are similar in size and scope, but when it comes to a competitive analysis, it's essential to look at your business from the customers' perspective.

Indeed, it's also necessary to consider "perceived" competition. These are retail stores or businesses that customers *believe* market what you sell—even though this may not be the case. For example, a custom cabinetmaker would offer higher-end options for upscale homeowners than in-stock, ready-made cabinets sold at a nearby home-improvement center. However, when conducting a competitive analysis, the cabinetmaker must still evaluate the home-improvement center's marketing tactics as they relate directly to cabinets, because customers will perceive the superstore's products as an alternative to the custom-made options.

Gather all competitive materials. Your next step is to acquire your competitors' marketing materials. This should include samples of their ads from search engines, Web sites, magazines, newspapers, Yellow Pages, and other directories. Collect any articles about them, print out their Web pages, and request their brochures, sell sheets, and all other printed marketing materials. You can even tape their TV and radio spots if they use broadcast media.

When it comes to scoping out retail competition, never overlook the benefits of mystery shopping. It's standard practice among the most successful retail operators. Simply by visiting your competitors during various times of the day, you'll get a feel for how they live up to their marketing promises, as well as insights that will provide helpful information for other aspects of your operation, from your product mix through pricing.

Analyze the key marketing elements. What's the purpose of gathering all this material and information? It's *not* so that you can copy it. In fact, that would cause serious repercussions for two important reasons. First, me-too marketing is lackluster at best and generally fails to produce results. Second, you never want to run afoul of copyright laws.

Learning everything you can about the way your competition markets provides essential clues to your own path to marketing success. You can identify the primary tactics used within your market niche to communicate with your target audience, and by learning what your competitors promise, you can develop a marketing message built around your company's unique benefits. What tactics and tools do the majority of your primary competitors use? Say, for example, you find that most of your chief competitors use folders with inserts as presentation tools. Chances are, you'll need a distinctive version of this tool—or something superior, such as a polished PowerPoint presentation and leave-behind—or prospects who take sales meetings with you as well as your competitors may find your tools lacking.

Decide how you'll position against them. Evaluate the materials you gather looking for key selling points. Don't be surprised if you see a lot of me-too marketing messages. There's just so much subpar marketing out there—in a field of 20 primary competitors, for example, you may find just 2 or 3 whose marketing really stands out and propels their companies forward.

What promises do your competitors make in their materials? Take a close look at the benefits they offer. These are topline message points, usually found in brochure headlines and the first sentence or two of print advertising, for instance. Then scan the features, or characteristics, of the products and services that are marketed. Based on this information, decide what you can offer that will add value and enable your company to position against its toughest competitors. But before you throw all your energies behind a marketing campaign built around your new key selling points, be sure to test whether the benefits and features that you believe distinguish your company from its field of competition are considered highly desirable by your target audience. This is where the low-cost research you learned about in Chapter 9 will come in handy.

Write a Hardworking Plan

With your competitive analysis complete, you're ready to write your marketing plan. Some small-business owners may find this intimidating. But don't worry, there's no need to write an elaborate tome. If you're creating your marketing plan for in-house use, what matters most is that you produce a hardworking document you can use to project your activity and measure your progress. Just follow my formula for a five-part plan using clear, short paragraphs and bulleted text. If you're creating your marketing plan as part of a business plan that you'll present to get funding from a bank or other institution, you'll need to flesh out each section with enough information to enable a reader who knows very little about your business to understand how marketing will be used to produce the sales necessary to repay the borrowed funds.

Your plan should be composed of the following five sections:

1. Situation analysis. This is an overview of your company's current situation, factoring in such elements as competition, staffing, new product development, your position in the marketplace, and even any changes in government regulations or the economy that may affect your business. Business schools teach students how to perform a SWOT (strengths, weaknesses, opportunities, and threats) analysis, and you may find it a handy exercise to complete to present a well-rounded snapshot of your company's present-day situation. Strengths and weaknesses apply to the internal workings of your business, and opportunities and threats relate to external elements.

To determine your company's **strengths,** ask yourself the following questions:

- How does what you offer compare with what's available from your competitors?
- If you offer products, how are they different or superior?
- Do you offer a service that others don't?

- In what ways is your company more expert or your scope of service more comprehensive?
- Do you have a strong position in the marketplace?
- Do you have an established brand or company image?
- Do you have a strong and expert sales force?

It's often easier to describe one's **weaknesses** than one's strengths. For example, do you have heavy competition or an uneducated market? Are you undercapitalized or understaffed, or do you have a product that's in danger of becoming obsolete? Any of these characteristics would represent company weaknesses that your marketing plan must overcome.

The **opportunities** section of your SWOT analysis challenges you to look outside your company at the marketplace. Some elements that would present excellent marketing opportunities include prospects who are educated in the kind of product or service you offer, the availability of potential marketing partners, established communications channels, and entry into a well-developed market.

External **threats** that may affect your company in the future are the final elements to factor into your SWOT analysis. While you don't have a crystal ball, you can project to some extent whether customers will continue to buy what you sell at the same or better pace. For example, do-it-yourself tax software may be taking business from small tax preparers who should be asking themselves what other forms of accounting they can perform. Consider whether there are alternate means on the horizon for accomplishing whatever your product or service does. Cable companies, for instance, are now being threatened by telephone companies as sources of entertainment over mobile devices, because customers will soon be able to store and listen to music on their mobile phones. Another example of a threat may be rising gas prices. As gas prices go up, so does the cost of operation for many small businesses that may have to cut marketing funds.

Taking all these elements into consideration, write a succinct, yet realistic situation analysis. As you move forward with the creation of your marketing plan, you must create campaigns and materials that capitalize on your strengths, overcome your weaknesses, maximize your opportunities, and face threats head-on.

2. Target audience. In earlier chapters, you learned how to create your own consumer target audience profile and how to write a concise description of your business-to-business prospects. Just plug in that short, one- or two-sentence description here.

3. Marketing goals. The next step is to create a bulleted list of your company's goals for the coming year. The most important advice I can give you is to make your goals measurable, so that you can accurately designate marketing tactics and budgets to achieve them. Plus, with quantifiable goals, you'll always know when you've successfully carried out your marketing plan.

Everyone wants to increase sales, but it's important to quantify this goal. Do you specifically want to increase sales by 20 percent per quarter, for instance? It's also a smart idea to assign deadlines for achieving your goals. Suppose you want to win a specified number of contracts from a new, seasonal target audience. An effective and measurable goal would be to achieve "Three new contracts by April 1, four contracts by July 1, two contracts by September 30, and four contracts by January 1."

4. Strategies and tactics. This section is the true core of your plan. It outlines your marketing strategies and the tactics you'll use to carry them out. Here are some examples:

The marketing strategy of the online dating service HoustonConnect.com is to reach area singles and induce them to participate in an online community that stresses fun and connects people with similar interests. It's important to note that this strategy has been developed based on a clear understanding of the marketing themes used by the company's competitors. According to HoustonConnect.com's president, the national dating service eHarmony.com promises to help members find their one perfect match based on answers to a questionnaire. HoustonConnect.com, which has plans to expand into multiple cities, has made the strategic decision to position against this larger competitor right from the start by creating a service focused on fun and building community among singles who share common interests. To put its strategy into action, HoustonConnect.com uses marketing tactics that include singles parties, radio sponsorships, a Web site dedicated to building community, and outdoor advertising.

One of the marketing strategies of Dance Distributors, sellers of shoes and apparel, is to reach dance students and motivate them to register for the company's catalogs and e-mail solicitations. And one of the tactics it used involved acquiring a direct-mail list of dancing schools from a well-targeted publication. The schools were sent posters with attached reply cards that induced students to sign up for Dance Distributors' catalogs in exchange for a special incentive.

In the late 1990s, Mary Hertert of Color Creek Fiber Art wanted to transform the nature of her studio's work from predominantly local art and design to commercial dyeing. Her strategy was to reach a national audience for this niche service through the Internet, and the tactic she employed to transform her business was paid search advertising.

To create your own strategies and tactics section of your marketing plan, briefly describe your primary strategies. For each marketing strategy, list the tactics you'll use to carry it out. If your tactics involve media, include a list of the publications or other media outlets. Next, create a time line for the execution of your tactics. This is very helpful because once you begin plotting the dates for execution of multiple tactics, you'll immediately see if you're taking on too much or too little. You can use software to schedule the execution of your tactics, or you can just note them on a desk calendar. What matters most is that you stick to your schedule. A marketing plan is only useful if it's a tool that guides concrete action.

5. Marketing budget. Before you consider your plan "set in stone," it's essential to attach costs to each of your marketing tactics. This may take a bit of work, because you'll have to contact vendors to gather pricing information on everything from printing through media space. As you price the execution of your chosen marketing tactics, you can adjust your plan by scaling back on the number of different tactics you'll employ until you've focused on a core group that you can undertake with sufficient frequency to achieve successful results. As you now know, you can use many different types of tactics to carry out a single strategy, and some are virtually free while others are higher-cost. Focus on a core group of tactics that fits your present budget and goals, then as your business expands you can adjust by taking on others that cost a bit more.

One of the chief advantages of being a small-business owner is that you can change direction on a dime. Unlike major businesses, which have layers of decision makers and often lumber on in a single-minded direction much longer than is profitable, you have the advantage of being able to make quick assessments of your marketing effectiveness and take equally swift action to correct problems. Carefully track and monitor the effectiveness of every tactic and soon you'll know what works and what doesn't. By consistently using the right marketing tools and programs, you'll win the sales you need to grow your business. What's more, these smart and affordable marketing practices will help you take your business to the next level—and achieve the kind of success you can bank on.

Chapter 1

1. Forrester Research, "The U.S. Consumer 2004: Multichannel and In-Store Technology Report," quoted in ClickZ.com, October 6, 2004, http://www.clickz.com/stats/markets/retailing/article .php/3418001.

2. Dieringer Research Group, "American Interactive Consumer Survey," reported by InternetRetailer.com, October 6, 2004.

3. Nielsen//NetRatings and the MegaView Online Retail Service, "Internet Retail Report Card," quoted in a Research Brief from MediaPost's Center for Media Research, April 22, 2005, http://www .centerformediaresearch.com/cfmr_brief.cfm?fnl=050422.

4. DoubleClick, "E-commerce Site Trend Report," quoted in MediaPost's *MediaDailyNews*, August 18, 2004, http://www.mediapost .com.

Chapter 2

1. DoubleClick's 2004 consumer e-mail study, quoted in ClickZ.com, October 20, 2004, http://www.clickz.com/stats/markets/ advertising/article.php/3423811.

Chapter 3

1. WashingtonPost.com and Nielsen//NetRatings, a study of working women's media usage and buying habits, released March 30, 2004, quoted in MediaPost's *MediaDailyNews*, http://www.mediapost.com.

2. BIGresearch, "February Consumer Intentions and Actions Survey," March 1, 2005, http://www.bigresearch.com/news/ big030105.htm.

3. Pew Internet and American Life Project, "Search Engine Users," January 24, 2005, quoted in MediaPost, http://www. mediapost .com.

4. Dieringer Research Group, "How Consumers Use Media to Make Local Purchase Decisions," April 18, 2005, quoted in MediaPost's *MediaDailyNews,* http://www.mediapost.com.

5. The Kelsey Group, "AOL Debuts Local Search," February 25, 2005, quoted in MediaPost, http://www.mediapost.com.

6. MarketingSherpa, "2004 Search Marketing Survey," August 9, 2004, quoted in MediaPost's *MediaDailyNews,* http://www.mediapost .com.

7. ComScore Networks, quoted in a Research Brief from MediaPost's Center for Media Research, January 13, 2005, http:// www.centerformediaresearch.com/cfmr_brief.cfm?fnl=050113.

8. The Media Audit, quoted in a Research Brief from Media-Post's Center for Media Research, April 8, 2005, http://www .centerformediaresearch.com/cfmr_brief.cfm?fnl=050408.

9. Pew Internet and American Life Project in conjunction with BuzzMetrics and Dr. Michael Cornfield, quoted in MediaPost's *MediaDailyNews,* May 25, 2005, http://www.mediapost.com.

10. CNN/USA Today/Gallup poll, conducted December 2004, quoted in a Research Brief from MediaPost's Center for Media Research, March 22, 2005, http://www.centerformediaresearch.com/ cfmr_brief.cfm?fnl=050322.

Chapter 6

1. The Direct Marketing Association, "2004 Response Rate Report," October 17, 2004, http://www.the-dma.org/cgi/dispnewsstand ?article=2891.

Chapter 7

1. DoubleClick's 2004 consumer e-mail study, quoted in ClickZ.com, October 20, 2004, http://www.clickz.com/stats/markets/advertising/article.php/3423811.

Chapter 9

1. Published quarterly by the Simon S. Selig, Jr. Center for Economic Growth, the University of Georgia, Jeffrey M. Humphreys, "The Multicultural Economy 2003, America's Minority Buying Power," quoted in a Research Brief from MediaPost's Center for Media Research, October 24, 2003, http://www.centerformediaresearch.com/cfmr_brief.cfm?fnl=031024.

2. Research Data Design (RDD), "Pulso Hispano Report," conducted July/August 2002, quoted in a Research Brief from MediaPost's Center for Media Research, October 7, 2002, http://www.mediapost.com.

3. People en Espanol, "Hispanic Opinion Tracker Survey," conducted in January and February 2005, quoted in AdAge.com, July 18, 2005, http://adage.com/news.cms?newsId=45575.

4. Arbitron, "Black Radio Today," quoted in a Research Brief from MediaPost's Center for Media Research, February 15, 2005, http://www.centerformediaresearch.com/cfmr_brief.cfm?fnl=050215.

5. New California Media poll conducted by Bendixen & Associates, "Ethnic Media in America: The Giant Hidden in Plain Sight," June 7, 2005, http://www.ncmonline.com.

6. Roslow Research Group, quoted in a Research Brief entitled "Speak the Language," from MediaPost's Center for Media Research, July 25, 2002, http://www.mediapost.com.

7. New California Media poll conducted by Bendixen & Associates, "Ethnic Media in America: the Giant Hidden in Plain Sight," June 7, 2005, http://www.ncmonline.com.

8. Arbitron, "Power of Hispanic Consumers Study 2004–2005," quoted in a Research Brief from MediaPost's Center for

Media Research, March 3, 2005, http://www.centerformediaresearch.com/cfmr_brief.cfm?fnl=050303.

Chapter 10

1. Arbitron, total radio listing estimates, quoted in a Research Brief from MediaPost's Center for Media Research, February 14, 2005, http://www.centerformediaresearch.com.

2. Burke study reported by the Radio Advertising Bureau, "Quick Guide to Dispelling the Eight Major Myths about Radio," http://www.rab.com.

3. Dynamics Logic's CrossMedia Research, an analysis of eight cross-media studies utilizing the three media, quoted in MediaPost's *MediaDailyNews*, September 24, 2004, http://www.mediapost.com/PrintFriend.cfm?articleId=270593.

Chapter 11

1. Cinema Advertising Council, "Nielsen Cinema Audience Report," September 2004, http://www.cinemaadcouncil.org.

2. TNS sponsored by Screenvision, based on a November 2004 survey of 2,000 moviegoers in New York City, Chicago, Denver, Seattle, Houston, and Charlotte, quoted in MediaPost's *MediaDailyNews*, April 19, 2005, http://www.mediapost.com.

3. Jack Morton Worldwide, "Experiential Marketing: New Consumer Research," quoted in *Jack Morton's Bimonthly Newsletter of Experiential Marketing*, June 14, 2005, http://www.jackmorton.com/360/industry_insight/jun05_industryin.asp.

4. Ibid.